A Time for Good News

Reflections on the Gospel for people on the go, Year A

Herbert O'Driscoll

Anglican Book Centre
Toronto, Canada

1990
Anglican Book Centre
600 Jarvis Street
Toronto, Ontario
Canada M4Y 2J6

Typesetting by Jay Tee Graphics Ltd.

Canadian Cataloguing in Publication Data

O'Driscoll, Herbert, 1928-
  A time for good news

ISBN 0-921846-07-X (Year A, v. 1)

1. Bible. N.T. Gospels – Liturgical lessons,
English – Meditations. 2. Church year meditations.
I. Title.

BS2565.047 1990   226   C90-093340-2

Contents

From author to reader . . . a few thoughts before you look further.

Every Sunday a great many Christians are not in church. Some are in bed, some on the ski slopes. Some are catching up at the office, some are watching television, others are trying to unwind after a gruelling week. There are many who have no choice but to be at work as businesses increasingly open on Sunday.

Not all of these folk are necessarily sinners and backsliders. Some are fed up with the church and wish it were otherwise, although if they were asked what they meant by ''otherwise'' they would probably be hard put to answer. Some want to give time to being a family, and since it has become too much effort to face the arguments about churchgoing, they have decided to give up the arguing and to settle for some quality time together doing other things. Some genuinely need to get out from under and head out of town.

The point I want to make is that not going to church on Sunday does not necessarily mean that one is not willing to be drawn to the things of God that day. So I want to offer this little resource. It can be used anywhere. It will take less than ten minutes to read each portion.

Every Sunday a special part of the Gospel is read in church. It's easy to forget that the meaning of the word *gospel* is *good news*. God knows, all of us could do with more good news these days. So why not get one of these little books and put it somewhere reachable. Put it in the driver's door of the car, or in your under-the-seat flight bag, or in your back pack, or beside your bed. You might even want to buy two and give one to a friend or a spouse or a fiancé. If you are a priest in a parish you might consider buying a number and using them in various ways that might very well be good investments in the best sense of that word. They could be used as small gifts when someone leaves the parish, as a thank-you to an outgoing vestry member or warden, as a give-away to those many people on the parish list whom you know are marginal to the parish's life but who might with a little encouragement be part of something worthwhile again. Perhaps one could be left as a small gift during a parish visit. In short, this little book just might be able to be that much talked-of and seldom discovered thing — an evangelistic resource! When they baptized you and me they didn't make us part of an organization. We became part of a body. They call it, as you probably know well, the body of Christ. It's beautiful and ancient, and deep down it can tell us who we are when we feel rather at sea, and it can help to put us back together again when we think we might be about to come apart at the seams from pressure or tension or sorrow or many other things. We may not have thought about it in those terms for a very long time. Maybe we should. It might become rich and vital and lovely for us again.

By the way, the church year, or the order in which Sundays come in a year, can seem a little complicated. If you are not sure what Sunday it is you could lift the phone and ask someone at the church. The readings for Sundays are arranged in a three-year cycle; Year A always begins on the First Sunday of Advent in those years evenly divisible by three (1989, 1992, etc.). This book contains Gospel readings and reflections for Year A; books will follow for Years B and C.

For now, try this. Read one or two. You might find yourself linked back with some good things that you have lost under a lot of other things that have filled up life. Finding them again might make a lot of difference. In any case. . .

Blessings to you.

Herbert O'Driscoll
Christ Church, Elbow Park
Calgary, 1990

First Sunday of Advent

36"But of that day and hour no one knows, not even the angels of heaven, nor the Son, but the Father only. 37As were the days of Noah, so will be the coming of the Son of man. 38For as in those days before the flood they were eating and drinking, marrying and giving in marriage, until the day when Noah entered the ark, 39and they did not know until the flood came and swept them all away, so will be the coming of the Son of man. 40Then two men will be in the field; one is taken and one is left. 41Two women will be grinding at the mill; one is taken and one is left. 42Watch therefore, for you do not know on what day your Lord is coming. 43But know this, that if the householder had known in what part of the night the thief was coming, he would have watched and would not have let his house be broken into. 44Therefore you also must be ready; for the Son of man is coming at an hour you do not expect."

Matthew 24:36–44

On what reality do we base our lives?

Life has always been unpredictable. Nowadays it is unpredictable not only in terms of our well-being and our health, but also in terms of our work. Vast changes in employment are taking place. Part of being a mature person is learning how to live with that unpredictability, to know that it exists, yet to trust that at the heart of human existence there is a creating God who in a deep and mysterious sense loves and gives meaning to human life.

In this Gospel passage Our Lord is talking about this unpredictability. He is telling us that all that exists, the universe, time itself, our human lives are under the rule of God and are finally accountable to God.

Our Lord refers to two very different attitudes we may adopt to avoid being accountable. We can live in a way that denies reality and responsibility. Such a lifestyle might include many things which in themselves are not wrong. We may, for instance, centre our lives around recreation, whether it be passive (watching television) or active (playing sports). Both are gifts of God but when life is totally centred on them, indeed when life is totally centred on any aspect of the self, then what is given as a gift can become a demanding lesser god which has to be served. Nowadays there are multimillion-dollar industries whose sole objective is to make quite sure that we centre our lives on our selves and our desires!

Our Lord's second quick portrait of life is the way we can deny reality by throwing ourselves totally into our work [vv 40–41]. The office or the plant or the store or the practice can become our world. But Our Lord then points out that there is someone who has a greater claim on us than our selves or our work. Self and work are necessary and good and precious elements in life, but they can never become the whole of life without diminishing it. Around them and within them there must be a greater spirit in which they are lived out. There are times we realize Our Lord's presence when we have great need or vulnerability, but, if we are wise, we will acknowledge his presence at all times. Then we will come to know that while desires may be good and work may be satisfying, with Our Lord as a reality in our lives both our desires and our work become more alive and more satisfying. That is this week's Good News.

Second Sunday of Advent

[1]In those days came John the Baptist, preaching in the wilderness of Judea, [2]"Repent, for the kingdom of heaven is at hand." [3]For this is he who was spoken of by the prophet Isaiah when he said, "The voice of one crying in the wilderness: Prepare the way of the Lord, make his paths straight." [4]Now John wore a garment of camel's hair, and a leather girdle around his waist; and his food was locusts and wild honey. [5]Then went out to him Jerusalem and all Judea and all the region about the Jordan, [6]and they were baptized by him in the river Jordan, confessing their sins. [7]But when he saw many of the Pharisees and Sadducees coming for baptism, he said to them, "You brood of vipers! Who warned you to flee from the wrath to come? [8]Bear fruit that befits repentance, [9]and do not presume to say to yourselves, 'We have Abraham as our father'; for I tell you, God is able from these stones to raise up children to Abraham. [10]Even now the axe is laid to the root of the trees; every tree therefore that does not bear good fruit is cut down and thrown into the fire. [11]"I baptize you with water for repentance, but he who is coming after me is mightier than I, whose sandals I am not worthy to carry; he will baptize you with the Holy Spirit and with fire. [12]His winnowing fork is in his hand, and he will clear his threshing floor and gather his wheat into the granary, but the chaff he will burn with unquenchable fire."

Matthew 3:1–12

We are responsible for the society we live in.

Sometimes we may be reading or watching television and we will hear or see something out in the darkened city. Perhaps a siren will wail. Or we may see on television a famine half a world away. At moments like that we realize that there is always an element of the wilderness hidden somewhere in the city of our world.

We tend to think of the city as a place where life is ordered, safe, controlled, always making things available when we need them. The wilderness speaks to us of the darker side of life. It is life as disordered, unsafe, uncontrolled. Deep down we know we can never entirely get away from the presence of the wilderness. We are constantly reminded of it in our cities and within our own personalities.

Today the Gospel introduces us to a man who has just come out of the wilderness. His name is John. He is forcing city people into the wilderness to hear him. John realizes that people in Jerusalem or in any other city like to think that the wilderness exists only outside the city. But he knows that the city is far from being as it should be. There is a great deal of smugness in its life [v 9]. Some people are using their positions of power and their resources in wrong ways [v 7]. John sees that the time has come to ask some very threatening questions about how the whole system of the city works, or indeed fails to work [v 10]. John knows that someone is about to come who will ask those questions, who will challenge, and call for great change. That person is Jesus of Nazareth.

Is any of this true of our own time and of our own society? Most of us can fall into the trap of believing that because we have our own role and place and rewards in the city then all is well in our society. If someone tries to point out some unwelcome truths to us we can feel angry and defensive. We don't find it easy to acknowledge that there are aspects of the wilderness in our neat ordered city. Poverty, injustice, racism, dishonest corporate practices, political opportunism, economic exploitation, are all pieces of the wilderness in the outwardly attractive city.

We can dismiss criticism as uninformed, troublemaking, even subversive. Instead we would be wise to remember that the questions being asked us about our society are sometimes being asked by the living Lord. Ultimately we are accountable to Our Lord as Christians in our society [v 12]. That is this week's Good News.

Third Sunday of Advent

²Now when John heard in prison about the deeds of the Christ, he sent word by his disciples ³and said to him, "Are you he who is to come, or shall we look for another?" ⁴And Jesus answered them, "Go and tell John what you hear and see: ⁵the blind receive their sight and the lame walk, lepers are cleansed and the deaf hear, and the dead are raised up, and the poor have good news preached to them. ⁶And blessed is he who takes no offense at me." ⁷As they went away, Jesus began to speak to the crowds concerning John: "What did you go out into the wilderness to behold? A reed shaken by the wind? ⁸Why then did you go out? To see a man clothed in soft raiment? Behold, those who wear soft raiment are in kings' houses. ⁹Why then did you go out? To see a prophet? Yes, I tell you, and more than a prophet. ¹⁰This is he of whom it is written, 'Behold, I send my messenger before thy face, who shall prepare thy way before thee.' ¹¹Truly, I say to you, among those born of women there has risen no one greater than John the Baptist; yet he who is least in the kingdom of heaven is greater than he."

Matthew 11:2–11

Knowing the time to say an encouraging word

Sometimes we lose faith in ourselves, in other people, in our work, in our church, in life itself, in God. Usually most of us work ourselves out of such a state but sometimes we turn for help. Today's Gospel shows us a very fine and faithful man doing just that.

John the Baptist is in prison. He realizes that the chances of his getting out are slim. He wants to know if his sacrifice of freedom and perhaps of life itself has been worthwhile. He has trusted that Jesus is the one sent by God whom he expected. Now, in his fear and loneliness, John sends a message to Jesus and he desperately needs a positive answer.

All of us can get into various prisons. Prisons of anxiety, of fear, of depression, of illness, of unemployment, an unhappy marriage. The things we have always believed in seem no longer to be resources to us. Let's take one aspect of this feeling that can sometimes be experienced because we are Christians.

Today Christian faith is a precious gift which is not always come by easily. Most of our society is not in the least concerned about it. We must seek Our Lord as he seeks us in our time and society. But even after we have found him and come to faith, there can be times of spiritual emptiness when we are not sure what we believe, if anything. Or someone going through such an experience may ask us for help and friendship. How do we respond?

Look at how Our Lord responds to John's question. He responds positively. He tells the messenger to go back to John and to tell him the good and positive things that are happening. Why does Jesus do this even when he knows the evidence is mixed? Because he knows that there are times when one gives encouragement and affirmation.

There are times when everyone needs such encouragement. Likewise there are times when we should give it. Huge changes, often puzzling and dispiriting, are on every side, in family life, in the workplace, in the church. But some immensely creative and encouraging things are happening if we are prepared to look for them and to share ourselves in them. Each of us may well have some very real burdens and problems, but not one of us is without certain blessings.

Is that a shallow and unrealistic way to look at things? It was obviously not so for Our Lord. So let us encourage others and receive encouragement ourselves. That's the Good News for this week.

Fourth Sunday of Advent

¹⁸Now the birth of Jesus Christ took place in this way. When his mother Mary had been betrothed to Joseph, before they came together she was found to be with child of the Holy Spirit; ¹⁹and her husband Joseph, being a just man and unwilling to put her to shame, resolved to divorce her quietly. ²⁰But as he considered this, behold, an angel of the Lord appeared to him in a dream, saying, ''Joseph, son of David, do not fear to take Mary your wife, for that which is conceived in her is of the Holy Spirit; ²¹she will bear a son, and you shall call his name Jesus, for he will save his people from their sins.'' ²²All this took place to fulfil what the Lord had spoken by the prophet: ²³''Behold, a virgin shall conceive and bear a son, and his name shall be called Emmanuel'' (which means, God with us). ²⁴When Joseph woke from sleep, he did as the angel of the Lord commanded him; he took his wife, ²⁵but knew her not until she had borne a son; and he called his name Jesus.

Matthew 1:18–25

God can help us to face things

There are some things so threatening or so painful that we are not only unable to respond to them, we are also unable even to speak about them. Sometimes we will even deny them, insisting that there isn't a problem. If we are lucky something or somebody will make it impossible for us to go on denying the painful or threatening reality. We will be helped to face it and deal with it.

This Gospel passage shows us what we need to do when we are tempted to deny the reality of things. Mary has told Joseph of the coming child. Joseph is appalled, utterly confused, probably feeling a helpless anger. He doesn't know what to say or do. Two possibilities occur to him [v 19] but he puts them both aside because of his love for Mary. However, he continues to brood over the situation [v 20]. It begins to invade his sleep and he dreams about the agony he faces.

In his dreams Joseph is helped to accept that this coming child is not a ghastly accident or a mistake or a threat; somehow it is meant to be. This child is a gift, a new life willed by God's Holy Spirit. Joseph himself is asked to name the child [v 21]. When he had reached that level of acceptance he was able to wake up [v 24], to come alive again in many senses, to accept Mary and her role and their relationship.

Each one of us is often like Joseph. We are faced with something which frightens or confuses or angers us. We turn away, and go deep into ourselves. We even cease to function adequately in either our relationships or on the job. We need help.

God will tell us that in surprising ways. Sleeplessness, nightmares, psychosomatic illnesses, turning to tranquillizers or alcohol, — all can be the messengers of God telling us we need the resources which God has prepared and can provide through others who care about us, who understand us, and love us. When we accept that help we come alive. We wake up. We find ourselves again when we name what we are struggling with. In time and with God's grace we can conquer it. That is the Good News for this week.

Christmas

¹In those days a decree went out from Caesar Augustus that all the world should be enrolled. ²This was the first enrollment, when Quirinius was governor of Syria. ³And all went to be enrolled, each to his own city. ⁴And Joseph also went up from Galilee, from the city of Nazareth, to Judea, to the city of David, which is called Bethlehem, because he was of the house and lineage of David, ⁵to be enrolled with Mary, his betrothed, who was with child. ⁶And while they were there, the time came for her to be delivered. ⁷And she gave birth to her first-born son and wrapped him in swaddling cloths, and laid him in a manger, because there was no place for them in the inn.

Luke 2:1–7

The circumstances of Our Lord's birth provide more than a long-ago and lovely story. They show us a deep truth about ourselves.

Sometimes it can be a good idea to try to get right outside what we are reading and look at it as a whole. If we do this to the first part of Luke's incomparable story we notice something very interesting. It starts out on a vast scale. We are at the spot of ultimate power in the world of that time. The emperor is making a decision that is going to affect the lives of everyone in the vast Roman empire. This he does and the machinery of the census begins to roll across the world.

But then notice how Luke puts a succession of decreasing lenses on his camera as he takes us across the empire. We move from Rome to Syria. Here there is the delegated power of the governor. Then we move on to a third place. It's a village named Nazareth in the province of Galilee. Here there is no power. There is just an ordinary man named Joseph. He doesn't make world-shaking decisions, he just has to respond to them. We've moved from power to powerlessness.

But have we? Notice how in verse 4 Luke refers to another royal house, a long-ago power before Rome. He refers to David, the King of Israel. It's as if Luke is very subtly saying that there is another kind of power involved in what is happening, and, if we are prepared to look very closely and probe the eternal ways of God, we will see what it really is.

So far Luke has given us an emperor and an unborn child. Could there be a greater contrast in terms of power and vulnerability? But wait. This is the work of God. We would be wise to look twice, to hesitate to accept things as they seem. Again and again we are told this great truth in the Bible, that the ways of God are not our ways and the thoughts of God are not our thoughts. We need to be told that again and again because we consistently forget it in our lives.

God does not work with the things or the people or the circumstances that may seem so right and appealing and desirable to us. Rome is a vast city and Bethlehem is a pathetic village, but it is in the village where glory is encountered. Caesar is mighty and Joseph is in that sense weak, yet it is to Joseph that is given the incomparable privilege of caring for the child of God. Mary is an unknown village girl yet she is the instrument through whom a reality almost beyond words becomes possible. As with Joseph, as with Mary, so with each of us. We are ordinary and all too human, yet the eternal God is prepared to use who and what we are in today's world. That is the Good News for this season.

First Sunday after Christmas

[13]Now when they had departed, behold, an angel of the Lord appeared to Joseph in a dream and said, "Rise, take the child and his mother, and flee to Egypt, and remain there till I tell you; for Herod is about to search for the child, to destroy him." [14]And he rose and took the child and his mother by night, and departed to Egypt, [15]and remained there until the death of Herod. This was to fulfil what the Lord had spoken by the prophet, "Out of Egypt have I called my son." [19]But when Herod died, behold, an angel of the Lord appeared in a dream to Joseph in Egypt, saying, [20]"Rise, take the child and his mother, and go to the land of Israel, for those who sought the child's life are dead." [21]And he rose and took the child and his mother, and went to the land of Israel. [22]But when he heard that Archelaus reigned over Judea in place of his father Herod, he was afraid to go there, and being warned in a dream he withdrew to the district of Galilee. [23]And he went and dwelt in a city called Nazareth, that what was spoken by the prophets might be fulfilled, "He shall be called a Nazarene."

Matthew 2:13–15, 19–23

We must respond to life with decisions and actions.

All of us have to live in a society larger than our immediate surroundings. The society may have many resources for us and for our family. We may use a daycare organization. Our children may take swimming lessons or some other classes perhaps at the local "Y" or a church hall or club. We will probably do a great deal of family driving to make all this possible.

But there will also be a dark side to the society around us. Joseph knew that in Bethlehem. Just as he knew that there was a threat to him and to his wife and child, so we may feel that certain things threaten us. Television is at the same time both a resource and a threat. Drugs may threaten our family. Our constant task is to make our children aware of the very real dangers of society without making them distrustful.

For Joseph and his family there was a very real and immediate threat from Herod, the local ruler. Joseph worried about that threat to the point of dreaming about it. There comes a time when we must find out whether a fear is imagined or based in reality. If it is real we, like Joseph, must act. Joseph fled with his family to Egypt.

One lesson of this passage is to teach us the absolute necessity of action, of taking charge of our fears and our problems. This may mean deciding to seek help. That is exactly what Joseph was doing when he headed for the shelter of the huge Jewish community in Alexandria. In our terms he moved to another neighbourhood!

Joseph and his family didn't stay there for ever. They made another decision, to move again because they sought their roots [v 20]. We also are searching for home and roots. Sometimes we do this by searching for who we really are. As we read this vivid and very human piece of scripture we realize that there are two great gifts we need to cultivate and give to those we love. One is the ability to act in the face of threats and challenges. The other is the sense that our lives are deeply rooted in terms of place or relationships or inner faith. Our Christian faith can be the strongest and most nourishing of roots, and it can be ours wherever we travel. That is the Good News for this week.

Second Sunday of Christmas

[1]In the beginning was the Word, and the Word was with God, and the Word was God. [2]He was in the beginning with God; [3]all things were made through him, and without him was not anything made that was made. [4]In him was life, and the life was the light of men. [5]The light shines in the darkness, and the darkness has not overcome it. [6]There was a man sent from God, whose name was John. [7]He came for testimony, to bear witness to the light, that all might believe through him. [8]He was not the light, but came to bear witness to the light. [9]The true light that enlightens every man was coming into the world. [10]He was in the world, and the world was made through him, yet the world knew him not. [11]He came to his own home, and his own people received him not. [12]But to all who received him, who believed in his name, he gave power to become children of God; [13]who were born, not of blood, nor of the will of the flesh nor of the will of man, but of God. [14]And the Word became flesh and dwelt among us, full of grace and truth; we have beheld his glory, glory as of the only Son from the Father. [15](John bore witness to him, and cried, "This was he of whom I said, 'He who comes after me ranks before me, for he was before me.' ") [16]And from his fulness have we all received, grace upon grace. [17]For the law was given through Moses; grace and truth came through Jesus Christ. [18]No one has ever seen God; the only Son, who is in the bosom of the Father, he has made him known.

John 1:1–18

As Jesus can be God's Word for our lives, so our words can bring life and joy to others.

We have all had the feeling of not being able to communicate something in a way that does it justice. We may have just heard a really beautiful theme in the background music of a movie or we may have just seen a terrific goal scored in hockey, the feeling is the same. We can't really communicate the wonder or the beauty or the excitement.

This is the problem John, the writer of this Gospel passage, faces. He and others had experienced Our Lord's presence for three years. Now he is old and is looking back. He realizes that he has actually experienced a continuing relationship with that same Lord since it all began beside the lake. Now he wants to express what that has meant. How can he possibly do it?

John decides to tell a story. To tell it at all he wants us to understand one great difference between what the words of God mean and can bring about and what our words mean and can bring about. For instance, when we say the word *star*, all that we have managed to do is to bring the concept of a star into the mind of the listener. When God says the word *star*, there, magnificent and awe-inspiring, real, solid, majestic and blazing, is a star!

Now let's take the words *light* and *life*. John tells us that God said these words and they took shape. The shape they took was a human shape; they became flesh [v 14]. An old word for becoming flesh is *incarnation*. The human shape in which God sent us light and life is Jesus Christ Our Lord.

John then tells us a most important consequence. The light and the life we see in Jesus can, if we so choose, become light for our lives. It can become a whole extra level of spiritual life [v 4 and v 9], and that is what we mean when we say that Jesus can be Our Lord and Our Saviour.

Something else comes to us from this passage, something about the importance of our own words. Our words cannot bring physical things into being but they can bring about both beautiful and terrible realities. A word from us can inspire someone, can encourage, can bring joy and hope. A different word can bring fear, hurt, anxiety, depression. A word said can never be unsaid. That may sound obvious but it is a truth we can never hear too often. As a Christian, each of us is called to make our words bring life and light, just as the Word of God brings life and light to us in the person of Our Lord Jesus Christ. That is the Good News for this week.

The Baptism of the Lord

¹³Then Jesus came from Galilee to the Jordan to John, to be baptized by him. ¹⁴John would have prevented him, saying, "I need to be baptized by you, and do you come to me?" ¹⁵But Jesus answered him, "Let it be so now; for thus it is fitting for us to fulfil all righteousness." Then he consented. ¹⁶And when Jesus was baptized, he went up immediately from the water, and behold, the heavens were opened and he saw the Spirit of God descending like a dove, and alighting on him; ¹⁷and lo, a voice from heaven, saying, "This is my beloved Son, with whom I am well pleased."

Matthew 4:13–17

Jesus renewed his commitment to God at his baptism. Do we need to recommit ourselves to Our Lord?

Decisions are difficult for us all. At about the age of thirty Jesus felt called to a decision in his life. His cousin John was talking to anyone who would listen about a new kind of world he felt sure was coming, a world for which people needed to make some changes in themselves and in their society. Jesus decided to go to John, to step down into the water of the Jordan river and to be baptized, intending this to be symbolic of the fact that one stage of his life was ending and another was beginning.

We Christians need to ask if there needs to be a moment like that in our own lives, a moment of deciding how to be Christian and follow Our Lord in a new way in our changing world. We may not have been baptized as children, or been confirmed in our teens. Even if either of these things happened in our early years we may still feel the need to find a way to say *yes* to Our Lord again. A friend might ask us to go on a Cursillo weekend. We might look at the new opportunity in *The Book of Alternative Services* to reaffirm our baptismal vows with other people at the Great Vigil service on Easter Eve (*B.A.S.*, p.330). Again, we might seek out a short course to refresh our knowledge of the Christian faith and end with our making a renewed commitment to Our Lord.

When we decide to do something like this we know that we are following in the footsteps of Our Lord himself. He knew what it was like to feel the need of renewing commitment to God. He made a decision and he acted upon it. He offered himself to God for God's service [v 13].

Notice what happened when Jesus did this. He became even more aware of God's Spirit being alive and active within him [v 16]. So will we. The spirit came to Jesus like a dove. A dove is the symbol of peace, in this case inner peace. In the coming of inner peace, we will experience the coming of the dove. Secondly, Jesus knew that he was being addressed by God. He knew himself to be in close and loving relationship with the God whom he addressed as Father. We too can come to know that relationship with God if we decide to act. We will find it through our relationship with Our Lord. We will find a deep peace. We will be called to serve. We will come to know who we really are. That is the Good News for this week.

Second Sunday after Epiphany

²⁹The next day he saw Jesus coming toward him, and said, "Behold, the Lamb of God, who takes away the sin of the world! ³⁰This is he of whom I said, 'After me comes a man who ranks before me, for he was before me.' ³¹I myself did not know him; but for this I came baptizing with water, that he might be revealed to Israel." ³²And John bore witness, "I saw the Spirit descend as a dove from heaven, and it remained on him. ³³I myself did not know him; but he who sent me to baptize with water said to me, 'He on whom you see the Spirit descend and remain, this is he who baptizes with the Holy Spirit.' ³⁴And I have seen and have borne witness that this is the Son of God."

John 1:29–34

We need to be open to the presence of Our Lord in unexpected people and at unexpected times.

Sometimes we look at things but we don't really see them. We can take in only so much and we all make our selections and decisions about that. But some things and people we neglect to our great loss. A Christian needs to pay attention to Our Lord Jesus Christ, to his life, his words, his spirit within us. This passage shows us a great man doing just that.

John the Baptist is a contemporary of Jesus, in fact a relative. John realizes that great changes are in the air of his time and society. He wants people to prepare themselves for those changes. But John sees more than this. His instincts tell him that Jesus, who has offered himself for baptism, is far more than just another face in the crowd. We need to realize that too. We as Christians need to be aware that Jesus can never be just another face in our own very crowded lives. We need to realize that for a Christian Jesus is *the* face, *the* person who matters. Notice how John says that Jesus "ranks before me" [v 30]. Does Jesus rank before you, his will before your will, his nature before yours?

John says that he didn't know Jesus [v 31]. In what sense is that true of us? Have I ever tried to grasp his life and ministry in a connected story? Or again, do I know a great deal about him without ever really knowing him as a presence in my life?

John tells us that what made the difference for him was his realization that a deep peace had descended on Jesus after his baptism [v 32]. Something seemed to radiate from Jesus which communicated itself to John as the power and the presence of God's Spirit. We can experience that in certain people. When we do, we realize that we are in the presence of the Holy Spirit, and therefore we are, through that person, in the presence of Our Lord himself. In our encounter with that person Our Lord is radiating his presence to us in our time and in our experience. We will feel this in the presence of a great Christian soul, someone like Teresa of Calcutta or Helder Camara of Brazil, but, if we are really open to the presence of Our Lord, we will feel it in the most unexpected people and on the most unexpected occasions. That is the Good News for this week.

Third Sunday after Epiphany

[12]Now when he heard that John had been arrested, he withdrew into Galilee; [13]and leaving Nazareth he went and dwelt in Capernaum by the sea, in the territory of Zebulun and Naphtali, [14]that what was spoken by the prophet Isaiah might be fulfilled: [15]"The land of Zebulun and the land of Naphtali, toward the sea, across the Jordan, Galilee of the Gentiles— [16]the people who sat in darkness have seen a great light, and for those who sat in the region and shadow of death light has dawned." [17]From that time Jesus began to preach, saying, "Repent, for the kingdom of heaven is at hand." [18]As he walked by the Sea of Galilee, he saw two brothers, Simon who is called Peter and Andrew his brother, casting a net into the sea; for they were fishermen. [19]And he said to them, "Follow me, and I will make you fishers of men." [20]Immediately they left their nets and followed him. [21]And going on from there he saw two other brothers, James the son of Zebedee and John his brother, in the boat with Zebedee their father, mending their nets, and he called them. [22]Immediately they left the boat and their father, and followed him. [23]And he went about all Galilee, teaching in their synagogues and preaching the gospel of the kingdom and healing every disease and every infirmity among the people.

Matthew 4:12–23

Deciding the right course in life needs God's guidance.

There are times when an event outside our lives, perhaps in someone else's life, triggers a response in us. We find ourselves making a decision that somehow wasn't possible or just didn't seem right until then.

We see this happening in Jesus' life in this Gospel passage. He has not moved yet into public ministry. However, he has recently accepted baptism in the Jordan from John, and has gone into the wilderness to work out what course he will follow. He has said *no* to a number of options which he felt were tempting but wrong. Now he has to decide what to say *yes* to.

As we all know, it is often much easier to say *no* than to say *yes*. In that situation, what should Christians do? We should present the matter to God in quiet simple prayer. Our Lord constantly did this. If a decision is not made during or immediately after prayer, we should assume that if we wait God will give us some sign. That sign will always seem totally ordinary and everyday. A friend may say something, a letter or a phone call may come, something we read (perhaps in Bible study) may suddenly point us in a certain direction.

It is very possible that Jesus saw John's imprisonment as a sign that he should set out for Galilee in the north. Perhaps the practical reason was safety; signs are hidden in the practicalities of life. Jesus realized that if God was pointing him that way, then God had something for him to do in Galilee.

God did. As soon as Jesus got back to Galilee he went to Capernaum, not back to Nazareth. Somehow he must have felt that that chapter of his life was over. To know this about our own lives is very important. Often we refuse to face the fact that a certain chapter is over; that can be very painful. We feel it when we leave home, perhaps to get married, and later when we move or follow a job to another city.

Notice what Jesus does first in Capernaum. He sets out to make relationships [v 18]. That is exactly what we should try to do at a new stage of our lives. There is another lesson here for a Christian. As we see Jesus encountering these four men at *their* work [vv 18, 21], we are being told that the same can happen for us, if only we are prepared to be encountered. That is the Good News for this week.

Fourth Sunday after Epiphany

[1]Seeing the crowds, he went up on the mountain, and when he sat down his disciples came to him. [2]And he opened his mouth and taught them, saying: [3]"Blessed are the poor in spirit, for theirs is the kingdom of heaven. [4]"Blessed are those who mourn, for they shall be comforted. [5]"Blessed are the meek, for they shall inherit the earth. [6]"Blessed are those who hunger and thirst for righteousness, for they shall be satisfied. [7]"Blessed are the merciful, for they shall obtain mercy. [8]"Blessed are the pure in heart, for they shall see God. [9]"Blessed are the peacemakers, for they shall be called sons of God. [10]"Blessed are those who are persecuted for righteousness' sake, for theirs is the kingdom of heaven. [11]"Blessed are you when men revile you and persecute you and utter all kinds of evil against you falsely on my account. [12]Rejoice and be glad, for your reward is great in heaven, for so men persecuted the prophets who were before you."

Matthew 5:1–12

What Our Lord meant by his vision of the kingdom of God.

Suppose we could ask Our Lord what were the most important things he wants to tell us. Certainly his answer would mention *the kingdom of God*. He constantly referred to it and told endless stories to illustrate it. "Listen," he would say, "the kingdom of God, or the kingdom of heaven, is like. . . ." Then he would choose something perfectly familiar to his listeners, and weave a story around it. Our Lord is showing how things would be if God ruled our personal lives and our society.

Always the attitudes and responses of at least one figure are those of a totally loving person. We see this very clearly in two of Jesus' best-known stories. The father is totally loving in the story of the prodigal son, as is the Samaritan in the tale of the wounded traveller. In such character sketches Jesus is drawing a portrait of God.

In this Gospel passage Jesus turns to the crowd and decides to share with them, and of course with us, what kind of world we would have if God's holy and loving will were fully reflected in human thought and action. What astonishes anyone really listening is the way everything he says seems to fly in the face of all we have come to think of as practical and possible and reasonable in our society!

In Our Lord's scenario it is the poor in spirit, not necessarily the confident and the powerful, who find the kingdom. Mourning is not necessarily something which destroys us. It can help us to discover the comforting love of others and so glimpse God's kingdom of love. Meekness, contemptible in our society, can often be deceptive. Underneath it there may be a great deal of grace and holiness if we can only be open to it.

On and on Jesus goes, giving us glimpses of a kingdom which turns our values upside down. Our society tends to think that being merciful is weak; Jesus says otherwise. Our society tends to think that being pure is rather quaint; Jesus says otherwise. Our society often thinks of peacemakers as interfering or unrealistic or even subversive; Jesus says otherwise. What this Gospel is telling us is that we would be wise to put our whole value system under the light of Our Lord's mind and spirit. The results would often surprise us, to put it mildly. That is the Good News for this week.

Fifth Sunday after Epiphany

¹³"You are the salt of the earth; but if salt has lost its taste, how shall its saltness be restored? It is no longer good for anything except to be thrown out and trodden under foot by men. ¹⁴"You are the light of the world. A city set on a hill cannot be hid. ¹⁵Nor do men light a lamp and put it under a bushel, but on a stand, and it gives light to all in the house. ¹⁶Let your light so shine before men, that they may see your good works and give glory to your Father who is in heaven."

Matthew 4:13–16

Our Lord shows us that affirming one another makes it possible for us to be responsible to ourselves and to one another.

One of the most wonderful things we can do for someone is to affirm them. We can help them to become aware that we think a great deal of them and therefore expect much from them. It is not enough just to feel this; we have to express it. This is where we often fail. Sometimes we fail most with those who are closest to us and whom we love the most.

Failing to affirm others can also cost a great deal in the workplace. In both family life and with our colleagues or employees we can for a long time assume that they are fully aware of our appreciation of their performance, so we fail to mention it. They do not feel they can ask us and keep wondering until the relationship is damaged.

Jesus was careful again and again to affirm people, making it clear that he thought they had a great deal to give if they only chose to do so. He was equally ready to question their motives and actions if he felt it necessary, just as we must if relationships are to be honest and real.

In this Gospel passage Jesus is surrounded by a crowd on a hillside near the Sea of Galilee. He turns to them and says something so affirming and generous that we use it to this day. Jesus says simply, ''You are the salt of the earth.'' But immediately he emphasizes that being the salt of the earth, being gifted, being useful, being creative, brings with it responsibility. The question then is how we use and offer what we have been given [v 13].

Again Jesus affirms his listeners. He says ''You are the light of the world.'' Once more he immediately asks us to be accountable to God for the gifts and qualities that may entail [v 14]. We may be the salt of the earth and the light of the world, but we will be so only if our gifts are directed out from ourselves towards others. If they are all directed into our selves and our own interests, then that which makes us salt and light is useless to God. The whole value of salt is its effect beyond itself. The whole point of light is to reach out and to guide.

Our Lord is quite direct and stern here. He affirms us but calls us to account for what he knows we can be and do. Affirming people does not mean that we ignore their shortcomings. But if we affirm one another when we should, we will enable each other to respond to the demands and the responsibilities placed upon us. That is the Good News for this week.

Sixth Sunday after Epiphany

¹⁷"Think not that I have come to abolish the law and the prophets; I have come not to abolish them but to fulfil them. ¹⁸For truly, I say to you, till heaven and earth pass away, not an iota, not a dot, will pass from the law until all is accomplished. ¹⁹Whoever then relaxes one of the least of these commandments and teaches men so, shall be called least in the kingdom of heaven; but he who does them and teaches them shall be called great in the kingdom of heaven. ²⁰For I tell you, unless your righteousness exceeds that of the scribes and Pharisees, you will never enter the kingdom of heaven. ²¹"You have heard that it was said to the men of old, 'You shall not kill; and whoever kills shall be liable to judgment.' ²²But I say to you that every one who is angry with his brother shall be liable to judgment; whoever insults his brother shall be liable to the council, and whoever says, 'You fool!' shall be liable to the hell of fire. ²³So if you are offering your gift at the altar, and there remember that your brother has something against you, ²⁴leave your gift there before the altar and go; first be reconciled to your brother, and then come and offer your gift. ²⁵Make friends quickly with your accuser, while you are going with him to court, lest your accuser hand you over to the judge, and the judge to the guard, and you be put in prison; ²⁶truly, I say to you, you will never get out till you have paid the last penny."

Matthew 5:17–26

Underneath surface feelings and actions there may be a need for reconciliation in our lives.

Jewish law, like any legal system, is immensely detailed. It has links to every conceivable element of life. This is not in any way criticism or contempt of that Law. What is truly magnificent about it is its assumption that every single aspect of human experience and thought and action is holy and comes under the rule and law of God.

Our Lord is very much aware of this when in this Gospel passage [vv 17-19] he speaks of the Law with deep respect. We as Christians need to be reminded that there is no area of our lives into which the lordship of Christ does not penetrate. For us Our Lord is the Law.

Notice how in verses 21-22 Our Lord goes much deeper than the surface. He points out that our actions come out of our motivations. These motivations are often far deeper than we suspect. They can be so deep inside us that we have not the remotest idea they exist. Our whole attitude towards someone, the way we think of them, the way we treat them, the way we feel in their presence, may be shaped by the fact that we are angry at them. Not only can the cause of that anger be unknown to us, but also we may not even be aware that we are angry!

Until we realize our anger and the reason for it our attitude towards that other person is going to be warped. This is what we mean when we say that Our Lord is able to go down beneath the surface of things and to discover the heart of the matter. We may need to do this in our own lives. There may be a relationship which requires us to find out the real issue below our surface actions and feelings. Until we do so our best efforts to improve the relationship will be defeated.

At the centre of any relationship, Our Lord tells us, is the need for reconciliation. Jesus saw people bringing gifts to the Temple to help them to feel reconciled to God. Quite rightly he points out that we cannot be reconciled to God until we are reconciled in our own deepest self. We cannot achieve that until we are reconciled in the relationship that is bothering us. To express all this in the simplest and most practical way, Our Lord is suggesting that it may be time for us to phone somebody or to write to somebody, better still to have a cup of tea or coffee or a drink or lunch or indeed anything! After that encounter, particularly if it results in even the beginning of reconciliation, the bread and the wine of the eucharist will taste even better! That is the Good News for this week.

Seventh Sunday after Epiphany

27"You have heard that it was said, 'You shall not commit adultery.' 28But I say to you that every one who looks at a woman lustfully has already committed adultery with her in his heart. 29If your right eye causes you to sin, pluck it out and throw it away; it is better that you lose one of your members than that your whole body be thrown into hell. 30And if your right hand causes you to sin, cut it off and throw it away; it is better that you lose one of your members than that your whole body go into hell. 31"It was also said, 'Whoever divorces his wife, let him give her a certificate of divorce.' 32But I say to you that every one who divorces his wife, except on the ground of unchastity, makes her an adulteress; and whoever marries a divorced woman commits adultery. 33"Again you have heard that it was said to the men of old, 'You shall not swear falsely, but shall perform to the Lord what you have sworn.' 34But I say to you, Do not swear at all, either by heaven, for it is the throne of God, 35or by earth, for it is his footstool, or by Jerusalem, for it is the city of the great King. 36And do not swear by your head, for you cannot make one hair white or black. 37Let what you say be simply 'Yes' or 'No'; anything more than this comes from evil.''

Matthew 5:27–37

As Christians all our relationships and all our actions are measured by the standards and values of the kingdom of God.

Anyone who thinks that Jesus was merely a nice, gifted teller of stories with a pat on the head for children and a winning smile for everyone can be brought up very short

29

by reading the Gospel. There are moments when one runs into something resembling a brick wall! Unless we understand the reason for that we will not know at times what to make of what Jesus says. We will be tempted simply to walk away from him in despair, feeling that what we have heard is totally unconnected with real life.

Jesus spent a great deal of his time telling us what human society and human relationships would be like if human will became totally obedient to God's will. If that were to be, Jesus tells us, the kingdom of this world would become the kingdom of God.

It is absolutely necessary for us to understand this if we wish to understand Our Lord. In much of what he says Our Lord is deliberately showing us choices and values which are diametrically opposed to the choices and values by which human affairs are conducted every day.

Here in this passage Our Lord is speaking about sexual desire and behaviour, as well as about human relationships in the context of marriage. Notice that Jesus first shows us how impossible it is for us to consider ourselves blameless in matters of sexuality, if only because we can never be in complete control of our thoughts [v 28].

When Our Lord speaks to us about cutting off our hand or plucking out our eye, he is telling us that we must take responsibility for our lives. There are some things in our lives we must deal with, even though to do so may be costly and involve sacrifice. If we do not deal with them they may destroy us.

Again, in the matter of marriage, Our Lord is saying categorically that it is for life, that anything less falls short of the ultimate demand of the kingdom of God. Our Lord says nothing directly to us about what we should do when continuance of a marriage proves impossible. Such issues the Christian community must work out in its own life, all the time trying to fulfil the ultimate command of responsible and faithful love which is the basis for all Christian decision-making and action. That is the Good News for this week.

Eighth Sunday after Epiphany

³⁸"You have heard that it was said, 'An eye for an eye and a tooth for a tooth,' ³⁹But I say to you, Do not resist one who is evil. But if any one strikes you on the right cheek, turn to him the other also; ⁴⁰and if any one would sue you and take your coat, let him have your cloak as well; ⁴¹and if any one forces you to go one mile, go with him two miles. ⁴²Give to him who begs from you, and do not refuse him who would borrow from you. ⁴³"You have heard that it was said, 'You shall love your neighbor and hate your enemy.' ⁴⁴But I say to you, Love your enemies and pray for those who persecute you, ⁴⁵so that you may be sons of your Father who is in heaven; for he makes his sun rise on the evil and on the good, and sends rain on the just and on the unjust. ⁴⁶For if you love those who love you, what reward have you. Do not even the tax collectors do the same? ⁴⁷And if you salute only your brethren, what more are you doing than others? Do not even the Gentiles do the same? ⁴⁸You, therefore, must be perfect, as your heavenly Father is perfect."

Matthew 5:38–48

Our Lord constantly calls us further than we think we can go, giving us his grace to respond.

There is a wonderful trait in us humans. We are always trying to push back horizons. We kept on until we climbed Mount Everest. But even then we want to do more. Recently someone has climbed it without oxygen. After that somebody who is in some way handicapped will climb it, or somebody who wishes to be the oldest person to reach the top! So we will go on, searching in other places, perhaps the ocean beds and the fields of space, for new horizons to push back.

Our Lord is like that in what he does for us and to us. Just as there are physical horizons which recede even as we reach a certain point, so Our Lord gives us moral and spiritual horizons which always remain ahead of us, calling us further and further to respond to his call.

For thousands of years there had been a standard which limited the extent of the revenge which a person could take on another. It said that revenge should reflect the extent of the original injury and no more. The image used in verse 38 is, "an eye for an eye, a tooth for a tooth." By doing this, even though it may sound cruel to us, the law was improving life greatly. Before that law, revenge could be unlimited. But Our Lord now takes even that standard and moves it to much higher ground. As we look at the four examples which Our Lord gives us in verses 39–42 we realize that the common factor in them all is that we are being asked to give over our will to that of another. We are being asked to respond in a way that seems totally beyond our capacity. Our Lord is in fact showing us what it would be like to respond utterly as the will of God would have us do. What is also important to see here is that this is the level on which Our Lord himself will respond when his time of suffering comes.

Everything in us backs away from seeming to give up control of our lives. We see Jesus' demand as an impossible one. But just as we are backing away from that demand we hear him make an even greater one! He asks us to love our enemies, pray for them who persecute us, do good to them who hate us. We read this and we feel overcome. But just as we feel this we remember something. We realize that he himself lived out every single one of these things. He did not do that because he is totally unlike us or has some magical resources we do not have. He did it in spite of his sharing our human nature. We can see these seemingly impossible standards being approached by great and saintly men and women, and we know that we are in the presence of greatness, that we are in fact in the presence of Our Lord. Their response to his demands calls each one of us to greater response in our own lives. That is the Good News for this week.

Ninth Sunday after Epiphany

21"Not every one who says to me, 'Lord, Lord,' shall enter the kingdom of heaven, but he who does the will of my Father who is in heaven. 22On that day many will say to me, 'Lord, Lord, did we not prophesy in your name, and do many mighty works in your name?' 23And then will I declare to them, 'I never knew you; depart from me, you evildoers.' 24"Every one then who hears these words of mine and does them will be like a wise man who built his house upon the rock; 25and the rain fell, and the floods came, and the winds blew and beat upon that house, but it did not fall, because it had been founded on the rock. 26And every one who hears these words of mine and does not do them will be like a foolish man who built his house upon the sand; 27and the rain fell, and the floods came, and the winds blew and beat against that house, and it fell; and great was the fall of it." 28And when Jesus finished these sayings, the crowds were astonished at his teaching, 29for he taught them as one who had authority, and not as their scribes.

Matthew 7:21–29

We need to watch the gap in our lives between promise and performance.

Human nature says one thing and does another. We begin in childhood. We say we will not play in the puddle but we do. As youths we say we will tidy the room but we don't. We will tidy it tomorrow or next Saturday or when the exams are over, but we don't. So the pattern goes on in our lives, always leaving a gap between saying and doing.

The Gospel says that Jesus knew what is in us human beings. Nothing is hidden, so we might as well save our energy spent hiding things we do not wish known to Our Lord. Our Lord had no illusions about our infinite capacity for saying one thing and doing another.

It is interesting to see that this point is left to the last in this sermon on the mount. Usually we put the really important things either at the end or at the beginning to emphasize them. If that is true then there is no doubt that Our Lord really wished to get across this message!

Our Lord knew that it is easy in spiritual matters to make all kinds of promises, to experience great emotion and great highs in our lives, to have wonderful visions in which we see ourselves doing this or that in the future. But all these feelings and promises can disappear in the face of the demands of daily life, its busyness, its temptations, its very real problems and sufferings. So Our Lord bids us watch very carefully the relationship between our saying and our doing.

Jesus tells us a story about two people who each build a house, one on sand, the other on rock. Both houses presumably look very much the same, each quite attractive and impressive. Each serves very well as long as the sun shines and the birds sing and life continues along pleasantly. But life changes, clouds gather, rain comes. Life becomes difficult, demanding, challenging. Stress builds. One house withstands the pressure and strain, the other collapses.

What Our Lord is telling us is that we very much need a rocklike consistency in our spiritual lives. One of the strongest components of that is to watch very carefully the gap between saying and doing, between promise and performance. The wider the gap, the less our spirituality has any real foundation. We will say yes to Our Lord today and yes to ourselves tomorrow. Our Lord understands this. His presence in our lives can help us close that gap. That is the Good News for this week.

First Sunday in Lent

¹Then Jesus was led up by the Spirit into the wilderness to be tempted by the devil. ²And he fasted forty days and forty nights, and afterward he was hungry. ³And the tempter came and said to him, "If you are the Son of God, command these stones to become loaves of bread." ⁴But he answered, "It is written, 'Man shall not live by bread alone, but by every word that proceeds from the mouth of God.'" ⁵Then the devil took him to the holy city, and set him on the pinnacle of the temple, ⁶and said to him, "If you are the Son of God, throw yourself down; for it is written, 'He will give his angels charge of you,' and 'On their hands they will bear you up, lest you strike your foot against a stone.'" ⁷Jesus said to him, "Again it is written, 'You shall not tempt the Lord your God.'" ⁸Again, the devil took him to a very high mountain, and showed him all the kingdoms of the world and the glory of them; ⁹and he said to him, "All these I will give you, if you will fall down and worship me." ¹⁰Then Jesus said to him, "Begone, Satan! for it is written, 'You shall worship the Lord your God and him only shall you serve.'" ¹¹Then the devil left him, and behold, angels came and ministered to him.

Matthew 4:1–11

When we face choices it is important that we know the basis on which Our Lord made them.

All of us have to make decisions. Sometimes it is far from easy. We go through a time of real struggle, sometimes actually feeling great resentment. Sometimes we become depressed by the complex choices before us, and sometimes we feel that we want to run away from the whole thing.

It may well be that Our Lord experienced moments like that. One certainly faced him when he went into the wilderness after his baptism. Actually the word *wilderness* may be the very best way of describing how we feel when we face making really important choices in our lives. All signposts seem to be missing; we don't know which way to turn. There may be unknown dangers if we choose one way rather than the other. One thing quite certain is that no choice ever provides the perfect answer. Jesus knew such thoughts well.

He had heard the call of God to public ministry, and had gone south to accept baptism from John in the river Jordan. Then he faced the difficult task of deciding how he was going to pursue the vision of God's kingdom which had been given.

Jesus tells us that the devil offered him at least three ways of building the kingdom. The first was to bribe people into following him [v 31]. The second way was to impress them [v 6]. The third was by reaching for power [v 8]. To each Our Lord said a resounding *No,* because he saw clearly that the devil was appealing to self-image and ego and the human longing for position and power. To build a ministry on what appealed either to his own ego or to the desires of those who followed him would be a betrayal of himself, of his followers, and of God. So Our Lord made another choice. He calls people to come to him and with him, not for what they can get but for what they can give of themselves to him, to one another, and to the world around them.

When we are facing a wilderness of choices it is important for us to be clear about the basis on which we are finally going to make our choice. Are we merely out for our own advantage? Do we merely wish to build our own image and position? If so we are failing to bring Our Lord into our choosing. But knowing that Jesus himself experienced the wilderness makes him our companion in our time of wilderness. That can make all the difference. That is the Good News for this week.

Second Sunday in Lent

[1]Now there was a man of the Pharisees, named Nicodemus, a ruler of the Jews. [2]This man came to Jesus by night and said to him, "Rabbi, we know that you are a teacher come from God; for no one can do these signs that you do, unless God is with him." [3]Jesus answered him, "Truly, truly, I say to you, unless one is born anew, he cannot see the kingdom of God." [4]Nicodemus said to him, 'How can a man be born when he is old? Can he enter a second time into his mother's womb and be born?" [5]Jesus answered, "Truly, truly, I say to you, unless one is born of water and the Spirit, he cannot enter the kingdom of God. [6]That which is born of the flesh is flesh, and that which is born of the Spirit is spirit. [7]Do not marvel that I say to you, 'You must be born anew.' [8]The wind blows where it wills, and you hear the sound of it, but you do not know whence it comes or whither it goes; so it is with every one who is born of the Spirit." [9]Nicodemus said to him, "How can this be?" [10]Jesus answered him, "Are you a teacher of Israel, and yet you do not understand this? [11]Truly, truly, I say to you, we speak of what we know, and bear witness to what we have seen; but you do not receive our testimony. [12]If I have told you earthly things and you do not believe, how can you believe if I tell you heavenly things? [13]No one has ascended into heaven but he who descended from heaven, the Son of man. [14]And as Moses lifted up the serpent in the wilderness, so must the Son of man be lifted up, [15]that whoever believes in him may have eternal life." [16]For God so loved the world that he gave his only Son, that whoever believes in him should not perish but have eternal life. [17]For God sent the Son into the world, not to condemn the world, but that the world might be saved through him.

John 3:1–17

We cannot always understand Our Lord Jesus Christ with our minds, but we discover that sometimes we have understood with our hearts.

Sometimes we just can't get something out of our mind. Nicodemus must have felt like that about Jesus because he risked a lot to see him. For a man of Nicodemus's prominence to be seen talking to a Galilean teacher was at the very least a professional risk. Like many of us, Nicodemus knew a great deal about religion and many other things, but he also knew that there was an empty space at the heart of his life. He longed for something more, so he came to find out about this kingdom of which Jesus had been speaking.

The conversation between them does not go easily for Nicodemus. First Jesus says that the kingdom coming into one's life involves being born again, coming alive in a new way [v 3]. Nicodemus tries to grasp that concept and fails. Jesus tries again. He says that experiencing God's kingdom is like feeling the force of a great wind. Actually, in the language Jesus spoke, the word for God's spirit and the word for the warm wind from the desert were the same word — *Ruach* [v 8]. But still Nicodemus doesn't understand. Eventually they part company. Yet, if we know the whole story of the New Testament, we know that Nicodemus's relationship with Jesus was far from being over. A couple of years later when the Sanhedrin (the governing body of the country, of which Nicodemus was a member) was planning to bring Jesus' work to an end, it was Nicodemus alone who challenged the planning. Not long afterwards, when Jesus' dead body still hung on the cross, it was Nicodemus who offered to help Joseph of Arimathaea to take it down. Both of these gestures could have been costly and dangerous for a man in Nicodemus's position and must have taken real courage.

We realize now that it only appeared that Nicodemus had not understood Jesus. Our Lord had reached his heart. We need to remember that. There is much about God and about Our Lord that we cannot understand. Nothing is so great and so deep and so holy as the birth, life, suffering, death, and resurrection of Our Lord Jesus Christ. But if we allow Our Lord and his Good News to become part of our lives, if we are prepared to encounter Jesus as a significant and real person whom we wish to know and to identify with, then we will find that we do understand. As Jesus said to Nicodemus on that long-ago evening, we will find that we have come alive in a new way and are aware of a refreshing and warming influence moving through our lives. When we do we know it as the Good News of Christ.

Third Sunday in Lent

⁵So he came to a city of Samaria, called Sychar, near the field that Jacob gave to his son Joseph. ⁶Jacob's well was there, and so Jesus, wearied as he was with his journey, sat down beside the well. It was about the sixth hour. ⁷There came a woman of Samaria to draw water. Jesus said to her, "Give me a drink." ⁸For his disciples had gone away into the city to buy food. ⁹The Samaritan woman said to him, "How is it that you, a Jew, ask a drink of me, a woman of Samaria?" For Jews have no dealings with Samaritans. ¹⁰Jesus answered her, "If you knew the gift of God, and who it is that is saying to you, 'Give me a drink,' you would have asked him, and he would have given you living water." ¹¹The woman said to him, "Sir, you have nothing to draw with, and the well is deep; where do you get that living water? ¹²Are you greater than our father Jacob who gave us the well, and drank from it himself, and his sons, and his cattle?" ¹³Jesus said to her, "Every one who drinks of this water will thirst again, ¹⁴but whoever drinks of the water that I shall give him will never thirst; the water that I shall give him will become in him a spring of water welling up to eternal life." ¹⁵The woman said to him, "Sir, give me this water, that I may not thirst, nor come here to draw." ¹⁶Jesus said to her, "Go, call your husband, and come here." ¹⁷The woman answered him, "I have no husband." Jesus said to her, "You are right in saying, 'I have no husband'; ¹⁸for you have had five husbands, and he whom you now have is not your husband; this you said truly." ¹⁹The woman said to him, "Sir, I perceive that you are a prophet. ²⁰Our fathers worshiped on this mountain; and you say that in Jerusalem is the place where men ought to worship." ²¹Jesus said to her, "Woman, believe me, the hour is coming when neither on this mountain nor in Jerusalem will you worship the Father. ²²You worship

what you do not know; we worship what we know, for salvation is from the Jews. [23]But the hour is coming, and now is, when the true worshipers will worship the Father in spirit and truth, for such the Father seeks to worship him. [24]God is spirit, and those who worship him must worship in spirit and truth.'' [25]The woman said to him, ''I know that Messiah is coming (he who is called Christ); when he comes, he will show us all things.'' [26]Jesus said to her, ''I who speak to you am he.'' [27]Just then his disciples came. They marveled that he was talking with a woman, but none said, ''What do you wish?'' or, ''Why are you talking with her'' [28]So the woman left her water jar, and went away into the city, and said to the people, [29]''Come, see a man who told me all that I ever did. Can this be the Christ?'' [30]They went out of the city and were coming to him. [31]Meanwhile the disciples besought him, saying, ''Rabbi, eat.'' [32]But he said to them, ''I have food to eat of which you do not know.'' [33]So the disciples said to one another, ''Has any one brought him food?'' [34]Jesus said to them, ''My food is to do the will of him who sent me, and to accomplish his work. [35]Do you not say, 'There are yet four months, then comes the harvest'? I tell you, lift up your eyes, and see how the fields are already white for harvest. [36]He who reaps receives wages, and gathers fruit for eternal life, so that sower and reaper may rejoice together. [37]For here the saying holds true, 'One sows and another reaps.' [38]I sent you to reap that for which you did not labor; others have labored, and you have entered into their labor.'' [39]Many Samaritans from that city believed in him because of the woman's testimony, ''He told me all that I ever did.'' [40]So when the Samaritans came to him, they asked him to stay with them; and he stayed there two days. [41]And many more believed because of his word. [42]They said to the woman, ''It is no longer because of your words that we believe, for we have heard for ourselves, and we know that this is indeed the Savior of the world.''

John 4:5–42

We cannot hide from Our Lord.

There is a great deal of unreality in the way most of us live. We can go a long way through life without ever facing up to certain things about ourselves we know very well should be faced. But what would happen if we met someone who was not prepared to allow us to get away with our games, someone before whom there was no use hiding.

The Gospel tells us of such an encounter near the village well of Sychar. It involved Our Lord and a very articulate and independent woman who, like us all, had things to hide, but again, like us all, was prepared to put up quite a struggle rather than reveal what was underneath her mask.

Our Lord triggered the encounter by simply asking for a drink. In that society that was far from being an ordinary thing to do. A man did not address a woman in such circumstances, and a Jew did not usually talk at all to a Samaritan [v 9]. Both rules applied here and Jesus broke both of them, probably because he had a strong intuition that something more important than rules, a human being's welfare, was at stake.

The next sequence of the encounter [vv 10–15] is a verbal fencing match. Our Lord moves the conversation to deeper spiritual things. She is determined not to, and, if we are honest, we know exactly how she feels. Only in rare moments, usually when our defences are down because we feel very vulnerable, are we prepared to express the depths of our life.

All during the fencing Jesus' deep intuition is at work. Suddenly he moves into the area of relationships [v 16], and strikes at the heart of her hidden world. Even then she makes one more effort to detour the conversation to the far less threatening subject of religion [v 20]. Relationships are deep inside us, religion can be kept outside if we choose. But Jesus does not allow her to succeed. He stays in the area of her problem and her pain [v 21]. Knowing too that this woman is far more real than she is pretending to be,

Our Lord calls her to face the reality of herself and the reality of the grace he can offer her. She shows her real worth by recognizing what he has been trying to do for her.

Our Lord challenges our urge to play games, to pretend, to refuse to face things in life of which we are either ashamed or afraid. However, Our Lord also offers us his grace to deal with those things. That is the Good News for this week.

Fourth Sunday in Lent

¹As he passed by, he saw a man blind from his birth.
²And his disciples asked him, "Rabbi, who sinned,
this man or his parents, that he was born blind?"
³Jesus answered, "It was not that this man sinned, or
his parents, but that the works of God might be made
manifest in him. ⁴We must work the works of him
who sent me, while it is day; night comes, when no
one can work. ⁵As long as I am in the world, I am the
light of the world." ⁶As he said this, he spat on the
ground and made clay of the spittle and anointed the
man's eyes with the clay, ⁷saying to him, "Go, wash
in the pool of Siloam" (which means Sent). So he went
and washed and came back seeing. ⁸The neighbors
and those who had seen him before as a beggar, said
"Is not this the man who used to sit and beg?" ⁹Some
said, "It is he"; others said, "No, but he is like him."
He said, "I am the man." ¹⁰They said to him, "Then
how were your eyes opened?" ¹¹He answered, "The
man called Jesus made clay and anointed my eyes and
said to me, 'Go to Siloam and wash'; so I went and
washed and received my sight." ¹²They said to him,
"Where is he?" He said, "I do not know." ¹³They
brought to the Pharisees the man who had formerly
been blind. ¹⁴Now it was a sabbath day when Jesus
made the clay and opened his eyes. ¹⁵The Pharisees
again asked him how he had received his sight. And
he said to them, "He put clay on my eyes, and I washed, and I see." ¹⁶Some of the Pharisees said, "This
man is not from God, for he does not keep the sabbath." But others said, "How can a man who is a sinner do such signs?" There was a division among them.
¹⁷So they again said to the blind man, "What do you
say about him, since he has opened your eyes?" He
said, "He is a prophet." ¹⁸The Jews did not believe

that he had been blind and had received his sight, until they called the parents of the man who had received his sight, [19]and asked them, "Is this your son, who you say was born blind? How then does he now see?" [20]His parents answered, "We know that this is our son, and that he was born blind; [21]but how he now sees we do not know, nor do we know who opened his eyes. Ask him; he is of age, he will speak for himself." [22]His parents said this because they feared the Jews, for the Jews had already agreed that if any one should confess him to be Christ, he was to be put out of the synagogue. [23]Therefore his parents said, "He is of age, ask him." [24]So for the second time they called the man who had been blind, and said to him, "Give God the praise; we know that this man is a sinner." [25]He answered, "Whether he is a sinner, I do not know; one thing I know, that though I was blind, now I see." [26]They said to him, "What did he do to you? How did he open your eyes?" [27]He answered them, "I have told you already, and you would not listen. Why do you want to hear it again? Do you too want to become his disciples?" [28]And they reviled him, saying "You are his disciple, but we are disciples of Moses. [29]We know that God has spoken to Moses, but as for this man, we do not know where he comes from." [30]The man answered, "Why, this is a marvel! You do not know where he comes from, and yet he opened my eyes. [31]We know that God does not listen to sinners, but if any one is a worshiper of God and does his will, God listens to him. [32]Never since the world began has it been heard that any one opened the eyes of a man born blind. [33]If this man were not from God, he could do nothing." [34]They answered him, "You were born in utter sin, and would you teach us?" And they cast him out. [35]Jesus heard that they had cast him out, and having found him said, "Do you believe in the Son of man?" [36]He answered, "And who is he, sir, that I may believe in him?" [37]Jesus said to him, "You have seen him, and it is he who speaks to you.'' ³⁸He said, ''Lord, I believe''; and he worshiped him. ³⁹Jesus said, ''For judgment I came into this world, that those who do not see may see, and that those who see may become blind.'' ⁴⁰Some of the Pharisees near him heard this, and they said to him, ''Are we also blind?'' ⁴¹Jesus said to them, ''If you were blind, you would have no guilt; but now that you say, 'We see,' your guilt remains.''

John 9:1–41

We can be blind to the many ways in which Our Lord can heal.

Almost all the really worthwhile insights in life occur gradually. Even when they seem to be there suddenly (falling in love), we spend the rest of our lives finding out what they really mean (what it really means to love another person and to be loved by them). In our relationship with Our Lord things are no different. We may have discovered him quite suddenly, a moment in worship, a weekend on retreat, a conversation with a friend. It could have been in a most ordinary and unpromising place. In C.S. Lewis's case it was on the top of a double-decker bus on the way to the Zoo! But wherever and whenever the moment it is always just a beginning. We may see him but we then spend a lifetime learning what knowing him means.

This Gospel passage is about a blind youth to whom Jesus gave sight. People who had known him blind were so astonished, they thought at first it was a look-alike [v 9]. They then brought some prominent people, some Pharisees, who seemed blind to the reality of what had happened. All they could see was that Jesus had acted on the Sabbath day and was breaking the Law. It followed that Jesus was a sinner, so he could not have been a healer! They simply could not admit that the youth had been healed. They called his parents. Was this their son whom everyone knew had been blind? Of course it was. The leaders turned again to the youth. He stuck to his story. It is interesting to see how the tough questioning affects the youth. It makes him even more aware of what he owes to Jesus, and more aware that Jesus embodies a power and a love and a grace that these people around him, for all their influence, do not have [vv 30–33]. In the end the group contemptuously dismisses him [v 34]. Jesus encounters him again and the youth recognizes an even greater authority that calls for his allegiance.

This story is about a person who came to see more and more clearly while other people became more and more blind to the same reality. Life is like that. There are those who recognize the power and love of Our Lord and there are those completely unable and unwilling to do so. In this story the Pharisees assumed certain things, such as the law about the Sabbath, not only to be true (which it was) but to be the boundaries of truth (which it was not). Today we can make assumptions that healing happens only in certain technical and scientific ways, all of which are valid. But we can also be blind to the hidden ways in which Our Lord can heal through our memories, our thinking, our emotions, if we are prepared to be opened to his healing love. Sometimes it is through a friend, sometimes it will be through a professional counsellor, sometimes a doctor. Our Lord has many ways to reach us. That is the Good News for this week.

Fifth Sunday in Lent

[1]Now a certain man was ill, Lazarus of Bethany, the village of Mary and her sister Martha. [2]It was Mary who anointed the Lord with ointment and wiped his feet with her hair, whose brother Lazarus was ill. [3]So the sisters sent to him, saying, ''Lord, he whom you love is ill.'' [4]But when Jesus heard it he said, ''This illness is not unto death; it is for the glory of God, so that the Son of God may be glorified by means of it.'' [5]Now Jesus loved Martha and her sister and Lazarus. [6]So when he heard that he was ill, he stayed two days longer in the place where he was. [7]Then after this he said to the disciples, ''Let us go into Judea again.'' [8]The disciples said to him, ''Rabbi, the Jews were but now seeking to stone you, and are you going there again?'' [9]Jesus answered, ''Are there not twelve hours in the day? If any one walks in the day, he does not stumble, because he sees the light of this world. [10]But if any one walks in the night, he stumbles, because the light is not in him.'' [11]Thus he spoke, and then he said to them, ''Our friend Lazarus has fallen asleep, but I go to wake him out of sleep.'' [12]The disciples said to him, ''Lord, if he has fallen asleep, he will recover.'' [13]Now Jesus had spoken of his death, but they thought that he meant taking rest in sleep. [14]Then Jesus told them plainly, ''Lazarus is dead; [15]and for your sake I am glad that I was not there, so that you may believe. But let us go to him.'' [16]Thomas, called the Twin, said to his fellow disciples, ''Let us also go, that we may die with him.'' [17]Now when Jesus came, he found that Lazarus had already been in the tomb four days. [18]Bethany was near Jerusalem, about two miles off, [19]and many of the Jews had come to Martha and Mary to console them concerning their brother. [20]When Martha heard that Jesus was coming,

she went and met him, while Mary sat in the house. [21]Martha said to Jesus, "Lord, if you had been here, my brother would not have died. [22]And even now I know that whatever you ask from God, God will give you." [23]Jesus said to her, "Your brother will rise again." [24]Martha said to him, "I know that he will rise again in the resurrection at the last day." [25]Jesus said to her, "I am the resurrection and the life; he who believes in me, though he die, yet shall he live, [26]and whoever lives and believes in me shall never die. Do you believe this?" [27]She said to him, "Yes, Lord; I believe that you are the Christ, the Son of God, he who is coming into the world." [28]When she had said this, she went and called her sister Mary, saying quietly, "The Teacher is here and is calling for you." [29]And when she heard it, she rose quickly and went to him. [39]Now Jesus had not yet come to the village, but was still in the place where Martha had met him. [31]When the Jews who were with her in the house, consoling her, saw Mary rise quickly and go out, they followed her, supposing that she was going to the tomb to weep there. [32]Then Mary, when she came where Jesus was and saw him, fell at his feet, saying to him, "Lord, if you had been here, my brother would not have died." [33]When Jesus saw her weeping, and the Jews who came with her also weeping, he was deeply moved in spirit and troubled; [34]and he said, "Where have you laid him?" They said to him, "Lord, come and see." [35]Jesus wept. [36]So the Jews said, "See how he loved him!" [37]But some of them said, "Could not he who opened the eyes of the blind man have kept this man from dying?" [38]Then Jesus, deeply moved again, came to the tomb; it was a cave, and a stone lay upon it. [39]Jesus said, "Take away the stone." Martha, the sister of the dead man, said to him, "Lord, by this time there will be an odor, for he has been dead four days." [40]Jesus said to her, "Did I not tell you that if you would believe you would see the glory of God?" [41]So they took away the stone. And Jesus lifted up his eyes and said, "Father, I thank thee that thou hast heard me. [42]I knew that thou hearest me always, but I have said this on account of the people standing by, that they may believe that thou didst send me." [43]When he had said this, he cried with a loud voice, "Lazarus, come out." [44]The dead man came out, his hands and feet bound with bandages, and his face wrapped with a cloth. Jesus said to them, "Unbind him, and let him go." [45]Many of the Jews therefore, who had come with Mary and had seen what he did, believed in him.

John 11:1–45

The life-giving power of Our Lord.

The home of Lazarus, Mary, and Martha in Bethany is a refuge for Jesus. They are dear friends. Our Lord hears that Lazarus is ill, but he does not go immediately. Then Lazarus dies. By the time Jesus reaches Bethany four days have gone by [v 17], and both sisters in their grief are angry at Jesus' seeming delay [vv 21 and 32]. We often experience grief as anger and direct our anger at those nearest to us.

It is quite clear in verses 4, 15, and 23 that Jesus realizes that this death is for him a moment of truth. Then Our Lord seems to come to a decision [v 34]. The story gathers power until the terrible and wonderful moment when Jesus, overcoming the protests of those around him, literally calls Lazarus back to life, and the frightening figure of his friend emerges into the light of day.

It is a deeply moving episode in Our Lord's life. As we read it, we cannot help linking this terrifying moment to the moment of mystery and majesty when Jesus himself returns as Our Lord, risen from death.

What is this scripture saying to us? It says many things but we can sum them up in one sentence. We are being told that Jesus can be Lord of all the many kinds of dying that we have to do in our human experience. "We die daily," said Saint Paul in one of his letters. We certainly do, and in many ways. We do some dying when someone hurts us; when we have to say a goodbye; when we betray someone or are ourselves betrayed; when we experience loss of any kind; when we must suffer pain. We do some dying when a child leaves home; when we lose a job; when we must move from a well-loved house to another; when we must move from our house to a nursing home. In every one of these lesser dyings we need a source of new life. We may need courage in the face of fear, hope in the face of despair, counselling in our depression, love in the face of some love being lost.

In every one of these circumstances we can feel as if we have entered a tomb. We can feel tied down, a prisoner of fear or despair or sorrow, cut off from everyone else, the sole inhabitant of our dead inner world. Our Lord can come to that dead world of the self. If we have known his friendship and have given him ours, we will be able to climb, perhaps laboriously at first, the steps to our recovery. Jesus as Our Lord can and does bring us back to life. That is the Good News for this week.

The Sunday of the Passion
With the Liturgy of the Palms

¹And when they drew near to Jerusalem and came to Bethphage, to the Mount of Olives, then Jesus sent two disciples, ²saying to them, "Go into the village opposite you, and immediately you will find an ass tied, and a colt with her; untie them and bring them to me. ³If any one says anything to you, you shall say, 'The Lord has need of them,' and he will send them immediately." ⁴This took place to fulfil what was spoken by the prophet, saying, ⁵"Tell the daughter of Zion, Behold, your king is coming to you, humble, and mounted on an ass, and on a colt, the foal of an ass." ⁶The disciples went and did as Jesus had directed them; ⁷they brought the ass and the colt, and put their garments on them, and he sat thereon. ⁸Most of the crowd spread their garments on the road, and others cut branches from the trees and spread them on the road. ⁹And the crowds that went before him and that followed him shouted, "Hosanna to the Son of David! Blessed is he who comes in the name of the Lord! Hosanna in the highest!" ¹⁰And when he entered Jerusalem, all the city was stirred, saying, "Who is this?" ¹¹And the crowds said, "This is the prophet Jesus from Nazareth of Galilee."

Matthew 21:1–11

Our Lord is always searching for points of entry to our lives and our society.

There are times when we know without any doubt that someone or something is making a claim on us and we have to respond. This Gospel passage shows Our Lord making a great claim, we have to decide how we can respond to it.

It seems as if Jesus had come to realize that there might not be much time left before the many forces ranged against him closed in. He decided to act out a very ancient prophecy [v 5]. Anyone who witnessed it would know what he was claiming, even though he would not say a word. He made his preparations and rode into the city.

How can we read this scripture so that it speaks to us? First we might think of our own lives as the city of which Jesus wishes to be king. The city of a human life has various gates, our mind, our heart, our relationships, our work. We can think of any aspect of our life as a gate or entry-point to the city of our soul, our deepest being. We never know through which gate Our Lord wants to enter. The point of our own poor efforts at spirituality is to keep as many gates as possible open for him. However, as Our Lord well understands, we are human. We cannot always keep all aspects of our life open to him. So from time to time he will choose a gate where he sees an opening and that gate may not be obviously religious! It could be our marriage, or the way we spend our money, or the way we treat our bodies. It could be anything. But when Our Lord enters through any one of these gates he is claiming to be Lord in the city of our lives. We have to decide whether we are going to ignore his claim or acknowledge it with our own "Hosanna." It may not be an excited shout. It may be a quiet acceptance of the fact that in this particular area we begin to serve his will rather than our own.

There is also another way in which this action of Jesus can speak to us. Our western culture can be seen as the city into which Our Lord is riding. This city acknowledges no king but itself, its needs, its power, and knowledge. In the face of this, Christ claims to be lord of the city. But whether we personally are the city or whether the city be the culture we live in, we are called to go out and welcome him. We do this by acknowledging that his claim is valid and demands our response. If we do this his coming will be Good News.

Easter — during the Day

¹Now on the first day of the week Mary Magdalene came to the tomb early, while it was still dark, and saw that the stone had been taken away from the tomb. ²So she ran, and went to Simon Peter and the other disciple, the one whom Jesus loved, and said to them, ''They have taken the Lord out of the tomb, and we do not know where they have laid him.'' ³Peter then came out with the other disciple, and they went toward the tomb. ⁴They both ran, but the other disciple outran Peter and reached the tomb first; ⁵and stooping to look in, he saw the linen cloths lying there, but he did not go in. ⁶Then Simon Peter came, following him, and went into the tomb; he saw the linen cloths lying, ⁷and the napkin, which had been on his head, not lying with the linen cloths but rolled up in a place by itself. ⁸Then the other disciple, who reached the tomb first, also went in, and he saw and believed; ⁹for as yet they did not know the scripture, that he must rise from the dead. ¹⁰Then the disciples went back to their homes. ¹¹But Mary stood weeping outside the tomb, and as she wept she stooped to look into the tomb; ¹²and she saw two angels in white, sitting where the body of Jesus had lain, one at the head and one at the feet. ¹³They said to her, ''Woman, why are you weeping?'' She said to them, ''Because they have taken away my Lord, and I do not know where they have laid him.'' ¹⁴Saying this, she turned round and saw Jesus standing, but she did not know that it was Jesus. ¹⁵Jesus said to her, ''Woman, why are you weeping? Whom do you seek?'' Supposing him to be the gardener, she said to him, ''Sir, if you have carried him away, tell me where you have laid him, and I will take him away.'' ¹⁶Jesus said to her, ''Mary.'' She turned and said to him in Hebrew, ''Rabboni!'' (which means Teacher). ¹⁷Jesus said to her, ''Do not hold me,

for I have not yet ascended to the Father; but go to my brethren and say to them, I am ascending to my Father and your Father, to my God and your God." [18]Mary Magdalene went and said to the disciples, "I have seen the Lord"; and she told them that he had said these things to her.

John 1:1–18

Jesus Christ IS risen TODAY!

We know immediately that we are in the company of a very courageous woman. What she did was both dangerous and frightening, and what she sees dismays her. The tomb is open and the body is gone. Her first instinct is to tell the other disciples. Two of them come and they too realize the body is gone. One of them leaps to the truth. The Lord is risen!

Mary is still searching frantically in the area. She meets a man she does not see clearly in the early dawn. Her response to his enquiry about her tears is to plead for the body she is seeking. The man quietly says her name and in that moment Mary knows she need look no further. She moves instinctively to hold him but he moves gently from her. Once again Mary seeks the other disciples. This time there is no cry of distress, only a statement so profound and significant it can be said only in the simplest words. Mary says "I have seen the Lord."

What does this moment in this woman's life say to us today? She came "while it was yet dark." As we late-twentieth-century Christians seek for Our Lord it is in many senses a dark time. In many circles it takes courage to acknowledge being a Christian. Sometimes the search is not easy. Jesus can seem to be no longer part of the world we live in [v 2]. If that feeling becomes strong in us we should do what Mary did, go for help. Join a group of others who are searching for him and for what he might mean in their lives [v 3]. Someone will take you further on the search than you can go yourself, someone whose vision is clearer, whose intuition richer, than yours.

Others can help but we must continue to search [v 11]. For Mary there comes an ironic moment. She doesn't know Jesus when she meets him as the Risen Lord [v 15]. We may be searching in our life for something lost, something we presume dead. Perhaps it is faith itself, perhaps a love lost, perhaps a lost sense of fulfilment about our job. We need to realize that the first question we might ask is "Why?". Asking that "why?" may be the moment Our Lord can meet us again.

Our Lord told Mary she could not hold him [v 17]. We cannot hold faith in Our Lord as a private possession. We need, as Mary did, to share him in community with others. There is another sense in which Jesus refuses to be our prisoner. Instead he grows and changes endlessly, and, as he does, he calls us to grow and change in our relationship with him. If we are prepared to follow him he will uphold us in the growing which he demands. That is the Good News for this week.

Second Sunday of Easter

¹⁹On the evening of that day, the first day of the week, the doors being shut where the disciples were, for fear of the Jews, Jesus came and stood among them and said to them, ''Peace be with you.'' ²⁰When he had said this, he showed them his hands and his side. Then the disciples were glad when they saw the Lord. ²¹Jesus said to them again, ''Peace be with you. As the Father has sent me, even so I send you.'' ²²And when he had said this, he breathed on them, and said to them, ''Receive the Holy Spirit. ²³If you forgive the sins of any, they are forgiven; if you retain the sins of any, they are retained.'' ²⁴Now Thomas, one of the twelve, called the Twin, was not with them when Jesus came. ²⁵So the other disciples told him, ''We have seen the Lord.'' But he said to them, ''Unless I see in his hands the print of the nails, and place my finger in the mark of the nails, and place my hand in his side, I will not believe.'' ²⁶Eight days later, his disciples were again in the house, and Thomas was with them. The doors were shut, but Jesus came and stood among them, and said, ''Peace be with you.'' ²⁷Then he said to Thomas, ''Put your finger here, and see my hands; and put out your hand, and place it in my side; do not be faithless, but believing.'' ²⁸Thomas answered him, ''My Lord and my God!'' ²⁹Jesus said to him, ''Have you believed because you have seen me? Blessed are those who have not seen and yet believe.'' ³⁰Now Jesus did many other signs in the presence of the disciples, which are not written in this book; ³¹but these are written that you may believe that Jesus is the Christ, the Son of God, and that believing you may have life in his name.

John 20:19–31

Doubt can often lead to a stronger faith and commitment to Jesus as Our Lord.

Some seemingly new things can turn out to be very old. If we sometimes wonder about the exchanging of the peace in worship we have only to read the opening verse [v 19] of this passage. There we witness Our Lord giving us the gift of this ancient Christian act. Why does he do it? To bind his followers to himself and to each other. Then he shows them his wounds, and tells them that he is sending them out in his name. Finally he passes his own spirit to them, his grace for all that lies ahead.

What does this mean for us? As we see in succession the peace of Christ, the wounds of Christ, and the spirit of Christ, we are being told that Christ's peace is very costly, but if it becomes ours it can strengthen our human spirit immensely. We all know someone who in spite of great suffering, or because of it, has about them an extraordinary peace as well as a power of spirit which is able to strengthen others.

Thomas is absent for all of this. When they tell him the news he refuses to believe it. Thank God for Thomas. It is Thomas, a man who spent two or three years in the company of Jesus, who gives us permission to experience doubt in our faith journey. But notice what happens when the Risen Lord returns. When Thomas realizes that the unbelievable is true he responds with total commitment. Our Lord's resurrection, far from being merely an interesting piece of information, becomes for Thomas a refocusing of his life. For Thomas Jesus is now Lord.

Maybe some honest, healthy doubting would be good for us who take Christian allegiance so easily for granted. If we do not doubt then we can never choose faith. We need to choose Jesus as Lord of our lives. He is not merely a fascinating historical figure. He is not merely a very wise man. He is not merely kind, nor merely a gifted healer, nor just a very good storyteller. For a Christian Jesus is nothing less than Thomas said he was — Lord and God. Is this true for us?

It's important to realize that Thomas was fully included in the commission Our Lord gave to his disciples. The fact that he had doubted did not lessen his value for Jesus. Our Lord knew that the person who struggles with doubt and wins through to renewed faith can be the truly strong and valuable disciple. Let each of us remember that in our doubting times. Doubt can lead us to Jesus as Lord. That is the Good News for this week.

Third Sunday of Easter

13That very day two of them were going to a village named Emmaus, about seven miles from Jerusalem; 14and talking with each other about all these things that had happened. 15While they were talking and discussing together, Jesus himself drew near and went with them. 16But their eyes were kept from recognizing him. 17And he said to them, "What is this conversation which you are holding with each other as you walk?" And they stood still, looking sad. 18Then one of them, named Cleopas, answered him, "Are you the only visitor to Jerusalem who does not know the things that have happened there in these days?" 19And he said to them, "What things?" And they said to him, "Concerning Jesus of Nazareth, who was a prophet mighty in deed and word before God and all the people, 20and how our chief priests and rulers delivered him up to be condemned to death, and crucified him. 21But we had hoped that he was the one to redeem Israel. Yes, and besides all this, it is now the third day since this happened. 22Moreover, some women of our company amazed us. They were at the tomb early in the morning 23and did not find his body; and they came back saying that they had even seen a vision of angels, who said that he was alive. 24Some of those who were with us went to the tomb, and found it just as the women had said; but him they did not see." 25And he said to them, "O foolish men, and slow of heart to believe all that the prophets have spoken! 26Was it not necessary that the Christ should suffer these things and enter into his glory?" 27And beginning with Moses and all the prophets, he interpreted to them in all the scriptures the things concerning himself. 28So they drew near to the village to which they were going. He appeared to be going further,

29but they constrained him, saying, ''Stay with us, for it is toward evening and the day is now far spent.'' So he went in to stay with them. 30When he was at table with them, he took the bread and blessed, and broke it, and gave it to them. 31And their eyes were opened and they recognized him; and he vanished out of their sight. 32They said to each other, ''Did not our hearts burn within us while he talked to us on the road, while he opened to us the scriptures?'' 33And they rose that same hour and returned to Jerusalem; and they found the eleven gathered together and those who were with them, 34who said, ''The Lord has risen indeed, and has appeared to Simon!'' 35Then they told what had happened on the road, and how he was known to them in the breaking of the bread.

Luke 24:13–35

Somewhere on the road we are travelling we are encountering the Risen Christ in some disguise.

Two people are heading out for a very long walk. It is no casual journey. They don't know if they will ever be able to bring themselves to return to the city they are leaving. They have watched someone die horribly, someone who meant everything to them. All the hopes and dreams which they had attached to him seem to have died too.

They are joined by a stranger and on they walk together, conversing as they go. The two begin to feel they have just met someone who can make sense of what has happened. They invite him into an inn for a meal. During the meal the stranger breaks bread in front of them, and they realize who is with them. But even as they do, he is gone.

This scripture is also about the journey for each of us. It may even be speaking to us at a moment when we, like the two, may be walking away from what is for us a dead Jesus, the sense of a dead church, a dead faith. If so we would be wise to have our eyes and ears open for the Stranger, because, somewhere and in someone, he is seeking us.

If we listen to what the stranger says on the road, we may hear what Our Lord wants to say to us today. Notice that "their eyes were kept from recognizing him." In our culture we have great difficulty recognizing Christ in the many forms in which he comes to us. We have been conditioned to recognize him only in specifically religious images. We need to realize that Our Lord can speak to us in any aspect of our daily experience. Our Lord is always in disguise.

Notice too how our Lord "interpreted to them the scriptures" [v 27]. Don't we need to know our scriptures far better than we do, particularly where the life and ministry of Our Lord are concerned?

Again, notice that the Risen Lord did not at any time force himself upon them. He waited for their invitation to have a meal [v 29]. We need to be among those inviting Our Lord into our lives. This might involve giving more time to the development of our Christian faith. It might involve our setting aside even a few minutes each day to be in his company, in silent reflection, simple prayer, or Bible study.

Finally Our Lord signals his presence in the simplest and most familiar of ways. He breaks bread. How important is it for you these days to be present with other Christians when Our Lord breaks the bread and pours the wine of the Eucharist? Maybe, like the two on the road to Emmaus, we need to return to the Christian community [v 33], to draw on its grace and to share our rediscovered faith. If so that will be Good News this week.

Fourth Sunday of Easter

[1]"Truly, truly, I say to you, he who does not enter the sheepfold by the door but climbs in by another way, that man is a thief and a robber; [2]but he who enters by the door is the shepherd of the sheep. [3]To him the gatekeeper opens; the sheep hear his voice, and he calls his own sheep by name and leads them out. [4]When he has brought out all his own, he goes before them, and the sheep follow him, for they know his voice. [5]A stranger they will not follow, but they will flee from him, for they do not know the voice of strangers." [6]This figure Jesus used with them, but they did not understand what he was saying to them. [7]So Jesus again said to them, "Truly, truly, I say to you, I am the door of the sheep. [8]All who came before me are thieves and robbers; but the sheep did not heed them. [9]I am the door, if any one enters by me, he will be saved, and will go in and out and find pasture. [10]The thief comes only to steal and kill and destroy; I came that they may have life, and have it abundantly."

John 10:1–10

A Christian looks to Christ for leadership and follows that leadership into every aspect of experience.

The world that Jesus knew was very familiar with the figure of the shepherd. Shepherds were absolutely vital to the economy. Ironically they were not paid well, in spite of the fact that their work entailed not only long hours outside but also a great deal of danger, particularly from wolves. The shepherd always led the flock and was responsible for finding pasture. Any suggestion that the image of the shepherd makes Our Lord out to be merely gentle and nurturing is very far from the truth. What is very significant about the shepherd's role is that it called for a person who was prepared to be gentle and tough, nurturing and driving.

In the language of this passage there are many would-be "shepherds" today who try to manipulate and exploit people for questionable ends. We might think of the thief and the robber of which Our Lord speaks as being among these people. A particularly false shepherd is one who will lead young people towards drugs. Such a shepherd comes, says Jesus, for no reason other than "to steal and to kill and to destroy" [v 10]. Jesus says of his followers that if they are wise they will not follow such a stranger but instead flee from him.

Our Lord now tries to get us to understand our relationship with him. As an image he uses the door which was in every sheepfold. Jesus speaks of our "going in and out" by the door which, in a spiritual sense, is himself. What this means is that a Christian sets out to use Christ's path or way, to do everything "through Christ," in short, to live life through Christ's grace and help.

Our Lord then says something we tend to miss in our culture. He says "I came that they may have life and have it abundantly." Notice that he does not say he came that we might merely have religion! Our Lord offers himself to us not only as the Lord of our religious experience but as the Lord of our total human experience. We hear this and we nod our heads in agreement but actually there is a great deal in our culture that fights this. The truth is that for a Christian Our Lord is the door through which one enters into every aspect of life, into one's office or shop or plant. Christ is the door through which a Christian enters into a theatre, a library, an art gallery, anything. What we really mean by saying this is that for a Christian no area of life is outside the guidance and the grace and the companionship of Our Lord. That is the Good News for this week.

Fifth Sunday of Easter

[1]"Let not your hearts be troubled; believe in God, believe also in me. [2]In my Father's house are many rooms, if it were not so, would I have told you that I go to prepare a place for you? [3]And when I go and prepare a place for you, I will come again and will take you to myself, that where I am you may be also. [4]And you know the way where I am going." [5]Thomas said to him, "Lord, we do not know where you are going; how can we know the way?" [6]Jesus said to him, "I am the way, and the truth, and the life; no one comes to the Father, but by me. [7]If you had known me, you would have known my Father also; henceforth you know him and have seen him." [8]Philip said to him, "Lord, show us the Father, and we shall be satisfied." [9]Jesus said to him, "Have I been with you so long, and yet you do not know me, Philip? He who has seen me has seen the Father; how can you say, 'Show us the Father'? [10]Do you not believe that I am in the Father and the Father in me? The words that I say to you I do not speak on my own authority; but the Father who dwells in me does his works. [11]Believe me that I am in the Father and the Father in me; or else believe me for the sake of the works themselves. [12]"Truly, truly, I say to you, he who believes in me will also do the works that I do; and greater works than these will he do, because I go to the Father. [13]Whatever you ask in my name, I will do it, that the Father may be glorified in the Son; [14]if you ask anything in my name, I will do it."

John 14:1–14

If we want to know the nature of God, we have only to look at Our Lord.

In this Gospel passage as Jesus says to his disciples "Let not your heart be troubled," he is actually touching the heart of our human situation. We are all deeply troubled about many things, about ourselves, our relationships, our future, our society. The list is long. In the face of this Jesus reminds us that our lives are not merely isolated and meaningless phenomena. Our lives are the creation of God, and for the duration of our lives Our Lord offers himself as our lifelong companion [v 1].

Jesus then speaks of the destiny of our lives. Life in this world is not all there is of life. This may seem a most obvious thing to say to Christians, yet the sad fact is that many Christians are so affected by the culture we live in that they no longer see their lives as being lived out as part of a greater life. We need to be reminded of this greater life by Our Lord's clear and most direct word in this passage [vv 2 and 3].

Thomas's sudden cry [v 5] is expressing something we all feel. What is the purpose of human life and how do we live it? For a Christian the response comes from Our Lord as it did to Thomas. The way we try to live our lives is Our Lord's way. The truth we try to find is Our Lord's truth, and the meaning we attach to our life is the meaning Our Lord attached to his. For Jesus the truth about life is that it is a gift given by God. The way to live it is to give it back to God in service day by day in all that we do. For Jesus this was the way and the truth and the life. So it is for a Christian.

We live at a time when there is much discussion as to who Jesus was and who he is for Christians. Such discussion will continue to the end of time because Jesus Christ is a profound and eternal mystery. But if we look at what Our Lord says in this passage to Philip we will hear one great truth about Jesus which we can hold to in any discussion. Philip asked Jesus to show him God. It is what we all desire, to know the essential meaning and source of life. But Jesus turns to Philip and tells him that he [Philip] has already seen a portrait of God in this very friend [Jesus] to whom he is talking.

Jesus is our window into the nature of God. Whenever we are conscious of the presence of Our Lord we are becoming aware of God's working within us. To know such things and to believe them, then to use them as the basis for our approach to life, is to have immense spiritual resources available. That is the Good News for this week.

Sixth Sunday of Easter

¹⁵"If you love me, you will keep my commandments. ¹⁶And I will pray the Father, and he will give you another Counselor, to be with you for ever, ¹⁷even the Spirit of truth, whom the world cannot receive, because it neither sees him nor knows him; you know him, for he dwells with you, and will be in you. ¹⁸"I will not leave you desolate; I will come to you. ¹⁹Yet a little while, and the world will see me no more, but you will see me; because I live, you will live also. ²⁰In that day you will know that I am in my Father, and you in me, and I in you. ²¹He who has my commandments and keeps them, he it is who loves me; and he who loves me will be loved by my Father, and I will love him and manifest myself to him."

John 14:15–21

For a Christian the spirit of Our Lord is already within. We have only to realize this and draw upon him.

Our Lord says simply that if we love him we will keep his commands. We are going to hear that again and again as we read our New Testament. In both the Gospels and the letters love is never sentimentalized. The Bible always demands that love be made real in action and that this pattern of action be in obedience to Our Lord's will. In that sense Christian love is first and foremost obedience. It is never merely a warm feeling!

Jesus continues by saying, "The spirit of truth . . . dwells with you, and will be in you." We say we believe this but if we really examine our spiritual assumptions we discover that we believe something rather different. We tend to think of Our Lord's Holy Spirit as something outside, beyond and above us, something which, if we are spiritually minded, we search for and pursue, something which we capture for a time and then lose again.

But Our Lord says categorically that his Holy Spirit dwells with us and will be in us. We already *are* the dwelling place of the Holy Spirit! To use another image of the New Testament, we could say that the light of God already burns within us. All of this is very different from the assumption of many people, that Our Lord's Holy Spirit may well be in certain great spiritual giants of the Christian community, but not in us ordinary Christians. We think that we have to settle for an odd touch of that sacred flame, an odd taste of the Holy Spirit. Not so. This passage gives us the assurance of Our Lord himself that however careless or halfhearted or ordinary a Christian may be, Our Lord is present in his or her life, not because our being is worthy of his entry but because he wishes to be there. In verse 23 Our Lord uses the imagery of homecoming. If we make a conscious effort to place our will under the direction of Our Lord's will, asking what his will may be in any given situation, then asking for his grace to do it, we will find that Our Lord becomes the familiar companion of our lives. He makes his home with us.

One more thing before leaving this passage. Our Lord says to us, "Because I live, you will live also." The simple yet tremendous truth is that people who have committed their lives to be servants of Our Lord in the world of their time live with a greater sense of meaning, a sense of being truly and fully alive. Try doing it. That is the Good News for this week.

Ascension of the Lord

⁴⁶[Jesus] said to them, "Thus it is written, that the Christ should suffer and on the third day rise from the dead, ⁴⁷and that repentance and forgiveness of sins should be preached in his name to all nations, beginning from Jerusalem. ⁴⁸You are witnesses of these things. ⁴⁹And behold, I send the promise of my Father upon you; but stay in the city until you are clothed with power from on high." ⁵⁰Then he led them out as far as Bethany, and lifting up his hands he blessed them. ⁵¹While he blessed them, he parted from them, and was carried up into heaven. ⁵²And they returned to Jerusalem with great joy, ⁵³and were continually in the temple blessing God.

Luke 24:46–53

We receive faith from Our Lord but we have to take responsibility for living it.

Some occasions in life that looked like endings turn out to have been beginnings. This moment when the risen Lord is visibly and physically present with his disciples for the last time is such a moment of ending and beginning. They have gone through wonderful and terrible times together. The relationship, as with all really worthwhile relationships, has been severely tested. Our Lord has known all of these disciples at their best and at their worst. But in spite of everything there is still the deep bond between the disciples and their Lord.

There comes a time in every human relationship when things must change. One of these times is when a group of people who have followed a particularly great and gifted leader must themselves accept responsibility for the future. The moment can be full of emotion, fear, gratitude, sometimes even anger. Why cannot things go on as they have been? Jesus is sensitive to these feelings [v 46]. First he tells his disciples that there is a purpose in all the events which have led up to this moment. Then he says that this must now be communicated to others because it has a message for the whole human situation, and that they who have been with him through it all have the task. They must have been appalled at the responsibilities involved. Realizing this, Jesus adds one more thing. He promises to give them the grace to do what he has commanded them to do.

All Christians have to come to such a time within themselves. We all have a relationship with our Lord by baptism, by worship, by some knowledge of the Gospel. Perhaps we need now to take full responsibility for that faith. What might that mean? Well, on that hill at Bethany Jesus spoke of the purpose of it all, the need to communicate it, the fact that only they could do it, and the promise that he would help them. Perhaps we need to put ourselves into that listening crowd. We might find ourselves asking what the purpose of being Christian is, of worshipping, of trying to pray, of trying to live out a faith. Our Lord replies that his birth, life, death, and resurrection are the secret meaning of all human experience. Dying and rising again is what it is all about. That needs to be communicated and we who have been told that great secret need to live it out in our lives. A difficult assignment? Very. But Jesus knows that; he actually lived it out totally. So he makes a promise, guaranteeing to us that if we are prepared to try to embody his experience in ours then he will help. Notice that they came down the hill "with great joy." That's the Good News for this week.

Seventh Sunday of Easter

[1]When Jesus had spoken these words, he lifted up his eyes to heaven and said, ''Father, the hour has come; glorify thy Son that the Son may glorify thee, [2]since thou hast given him power over all flesh, to give eternal life to all whom thou hast given him. [3]And this is eternal life, that they know thee the only true God, and Jesus Christ whom thou hast sent. [4]I glorified thee on earth, having accomplished the work which thou gavest me to do; [5]and now, Father, glorify thou me in thy own presence with the glory which I had with thee before the world was made. [6]''I have manifested thy name to the men whom thou gavest me out of the world; thine they were, and thou gavest them to me, and they have kept thy word. [7]Now they know that everything that thou hast given me is from thee; [8]for I have given them the words which thou gavest me, and they have received them and know in truth that I came from thee; and they have believed that thou didst send me. [9]I am praying for them; I am not praying for the world but for those whom thou hast given me, for they are thine; [10]all mine are thine, and thine are mine, and I am glorified in them. [11]And now I am no more in the world, but they are in the world, and I am coming to thee. Holy Father, keep them in thy name, which thou hast given me, that they may be one, even as we are one.''

John 17:1–11

It is easy to forget that Our Lord himself prays for us. What might that mean for our lives?

We know that Our Lord prayed constantly. In this instance John gives us a long and intense prayer offered by Our Lord for his disciples. It has all the intensity of a person who realizes that time is running out to say the things that need to be said in any intimate relationship.

"Father" is Our Lord's first word. It always was in his prayers. It expresses the intimacy with which he saw God. If we are wise the first word on our lips when we pray will name God as a loving parent, whether that be Father or Mother.

Our Lord continues with an insight about our lives as Christians [v 3]. Eternal life is not merely life apart from or following on this life. Eternal life is an ultimate quality of being alive which begins in this life if we so choose. It means living our lives with a deep and satisfying meaning and purpose, possessing what Christian faith since biblical times has called joy. Jesus says that the way to possess this eternal quality of life is to live in a relationship with Our Lord as friend and brother, knowing that that relationship links us with the love and the grace of God.

In a single sentence Our Lord gives us the reason for being alive. He looks back on his own earthly life soon to end and says that its object has always been to give glory to God. He has always seen his life as given to him to carry out a "work" which he sees as his special vocation [v 4]. In saying these things Our Lord is saying why each of us has been given the gift of life. For us too life is for giving glory to God in our daily living. It is for seeing that we too have each been given a special "work" or vocation.

Now Jesus prays for those who follow him; that includes each of us. He reminds us that he himself has not only spoken God's word but also that he has been God's word of love and life among us [v 8]. He wants always to be glorified in each of our lives [v 10]. To what extent is he?

Finally in verse 11 Jesus shows he is aware that you and I are "in the world," with all its challenges and ambiguities. He prays that we may be one, and that can have different meanings for us. Jesus prays that each of us may know the inner wholeness we all seek in life, also that we may feel at one with a worshipping community of Christians who know one another, share themselves in mutual trust, and serve together. That Our Lord prays for us is the Good News for this week.

The Day of Pentecost

³⁷On the last day of the feast, the great day, Jesus stood up and proclaimed, "If any one thirst, let him come to me and drink. ³⁸He who believes in me, as the scripture has said, 'Out of his heart shall flow rivers of living water.' " ³⁹Now this he said about the Spirit, which those who believed in him were to receive; for as yet the Spirit had not been given, because Jesus was not yet glorified.

John 7:37–39

Our Lord tells us that a what's-in-it-for-me spirituality is not enough.

C.S. Lewis said on many occasions that we simply must not try to understand everything Our Lord says in a literal way. For instance, he once pointed out that when Jesus said we were to be like doves he did not intend us to lay eggs!

That's a very obvious example of the kind of thing we have to deal with in this Gospel passage. Our Lord has a formidable task. He is telling us of the ways of God, describing for us what he calls the kingdom of God. Jesus is also describing God's dealings with us, how the Holy Spirit of God communicates with our human spirits. We are the creation of God but our spirits can wander very far indeed from that same Holy Spirit! It is this sense of separation which Jesus sets out to repair. To do so he speaks in a way which was very rich and helpful for his time and culture. He will constantly use the word "like," and he will always use a direct and simple image taken from ordinary life.

One day, while speaking in an area of the Temple, Jesus said, "If any one thirst let him come to me and drink." For a Christian this is not merely a long-ago statement to a long-ago group; Our Lord is saying this to us now. What does he mean?

In every human spirit there is a thirst for something. We thirst for relationships, for meaning, for love. Whether we know it or not we thirst for God. What Jesus is saying is both very simple and very profound. He is saying that a relationship with him as Lord is capable of helping us find those other things. Notice that Our Lord does not offer us a relationship with himself which of itself, in some magically religious way, produces what we thirst for. Instead we come to realize that a relationship with Our Lord helps us to approach the world and everyday life in such a way that we become capable of finding relationships, love, joy, and meaning in the things we experience and the people we encounter.

Notice however what Jesus says immediately afterwards. He points out [v 38] that anyone who does drink in his spirit must not do so only to satisfy his or her own longings [thirst]. A relationship with Our Lord is not for the sole purpose of what it gives us. We seek these things of Our Lord so that we in turn can be grace to others. Having gone to the spiritual well which Our Lord can be for us, we are then to be a source of nourishment for those with whom we come into contact. That is the Good News for this week.

Trinity Sunday

¹⁶Now the eleven disciples went to Galilee, to the mountain to which Jesus had directed them. ¹⁷And when they saw him they worshiped him; but some doubted. ¹⁸And Jesus came and said to them "All authority in heaven and on earth has been given to me. ¹⁹Go therefore and make disciples of all nations, baptizing them in the name of the Father and of the Son and of the Holy Spirit, ²⁰teaching them to observe all that I have commanded you; and lo, I am with you always, to the close of the age."

Matthew 28:16–20

In spite of all our shortcomings as individuals and as a church, Our Lord uses us to do his work.

There is a wonderful old story told of Our Lord returning to heaven after being with us on earth. Gabriel welcomes him and says "Lord, your work on earth is finished?" Jesus says "No Gabriel, far from it. My work has only begun." The surprised archangel says "Then what means have you left on the earth for concluding your work?" Jesus says "I have left a community of men and women." Gabriel looks rather doubtful and concerned, and says, "But, Lord, what if they should fail?" Jesus answers, "Then, Gabriel, I have no other way."

Try now to imagine ourselves standing a little apart from the group of disciples clustered around Our Lord in this Gospel passage. We become aware that there are only eleven of them. Matthew recalls this very fact as he prepares to bring his version of the Gospel to an end. Why? Sometimes as we read scripture a single word can communicate a great deal to us. Look carefully at the word "eleven" in verse 28. As we read the four Gospels we are always aware of the twelve disciples. But, as we know, something happened to break that complete circle. Judas betrayed Our Lord and went from the community. That means that by the time Our Lord's ascension comes, the moment Matthew is sharing with us here, the community has been wounded. But Our Lord stands within this damaged group and still gives them his great commission. He assigns them his work for the rest of time [vv 18–20]. Think of the level of trust that entailed.

We begin to realize the really Good News for us all in this. In many senses we Christians today are "the eleven." Each one of us, as well as the whole Christian community, has many and obvious weaknesses. Great differences and tensions abound. But look again at the Gospel. See how Matthew points out [v 17] the presence of doubts and differences and tensions in the phrase "they worshipped him but some doubted." We see that it has always been this way and it always will be. There will never come the perfect time or the perfect church. Always there will be reasons for doubt and differences. Our Lord knows this well, just as he knew it on that long-ago hilltop in Galilee. But, as on that day with that pathetic little group, Jesus does not hesitate a moment in giving us his work to do in our time. He accepts the reality of each of us and that of the whole church. He takes our strengths, our gifts, our individual abilities, as well as all the potential there is among us when we work together. He looks at us, understands us, accepts us. Then he calls us to do his work. That is the Good News for this week.

Sunday between 12 and 18 June

35And Jesus went about all the cities and villages, teaching in their synagogues and preaching the gospel of the kingdom, and healing every disease and every infirmity. 36When he saw the crowds, he had compassion for them, because they were harassed and helpless, like sheep without a shepherd. 37Then he said to his disciples, ''The harvest is plentiful, but the laborers are few; 38pray therefore the Lord of the harvest to send out laborers into his harvest.''

1And he called to him his twelve disciples and gave them authority over unclean spirits, to cast them out, and to heal every disease and every infirmity. 2The names of the twelve apostles are these: first, Simon, who is called Peter, and Andrew his brother; James the son of Zeb'edee, and John his brother; 3Philip and Bartholomew; Thomas and Matthew the tax collector; James the son of Alphaeus, and Thaddaeus; 4Simon the Cananaean, and Judas Iscariot, who betrayed him.5These twelve Jesus sent out, charging them, ''Go nowhere among the Gentiles, and enter no town of the Samaritans, 6but go rather to the lost sheep of the house of Israel. 7And preach as you go, saying, ''The kingdom of heaven is at hand.' 8Heal the sick, raise the dead, cleanse lepers, cast out demons. You received without paying, give without pay.''

Matthew 9:35—10:8

As Our Lord named his original disciples, so he names us to do his work in our time.

Nothing we read in sacred scripture is merely about the past. The event in scripture, past though it may be, is also very much with us in the present. In scripture Our Lord *is speaking* to us, not merely *has spoken* to people in the past.

In this passage Matthew has brought us to the point where Jesus realizes that the time has come to name those whose responsibility it will be to work with him on his mission. There is a hint [v 35] that the demands of that mission are getting beyond one pair of hands, even if those hands are the most loving and gracious hands ever to touch this world. We know that these people have already become disciples of Jesus [v 37].But now something more must be done. There needs to be an actual moment when these same disciples are given what the scripture calls "authority" [v 1]. This is not seen as an authority merely to give orders, which most of us like doing, but an authority to serve others, which we don't always like! Jesus then names the twelve, carefully and deliberately, and sends them out [v 5]. What does this deceptively simple scene say to us?

As a Christian, each of us is part of the Body of Christ. But there must come a moment when we ourselves freely realize what this means. We must own our baptism, and take responsibility for it. The experience we call confirmation is meant to help us toward that, but in actual fact taking complete responsibility for our baptism may not come for a long time.

We are already disciples by our baptism, but have we fully realized what disciples do? In verse 35 we see what Our Lord's work is. It is teaching, preaching, healing. We may not be called to do all these things. Teaching could be in many forms of handing on the faith, even if only to our own small children. But we teach by being who we are. Healing can include any act of service to another or to society.

We are named. How? In baptism. But we need to hear Our Lord name us again. It can happen in many quiet and unexpected moments if we will only listen. When we hear our name we will know what Our Lord wants us to do. Then, with his grace, we will be able to do it. That is the Good News for this week.

Sunday between 19 and 25 June

²⁴''A disciple is not above his teacher, nor a servant above his master; ²⁵it is enough for the disciple to be like his teacher, and the servant like his master. If they have called the master of the house Be-el'zebul, how much more will they malign those of his household. ²⁶''So have no fear of them; for nothing is covered that will not be revealed, or hidden that will not be known. ²⁷What I tell you in the dark, utter in the light; and what you hear whispered, proclaim upon the house-tops. ²⁸And do not fear those who kill the body but cannot kill the soul; rather fear him who can destroy both soul and body in hell. ²⁹Are not two sparrows sold for a penny? And not one of them will fall to the ground without your Father's will. ³⁰But even the hairs of your head are all numbered. ³¹Fear not, therefore; you are of more value than many sparrows. ³²So every one who acknowledges me before men, I also will acknowledge before my Father who is in heaven; ³³ but whoever denies me before men, I also will deny before my Father who is in heaven.''

Matthew 10:24–33

Our Lord experienced resistance when he challenged others. His Gospel will always meet such resistance.

For Our Lord life was sometimes very difficult indeed. We need to be quite clear about this because otherwise we go through life with a very unreal Jesus. In this passage Our Lord is talking to anyone who wishes to follow his way. That way was by no means palatable to everyone who came in contact with him. People tended to be either captivated or alienated. Some were so alienated that they were prepared to act out their hatred. They began by saying that Jesus' work was that of the devil [v 25]. Our Lord was under no illusions about the consequences for those who in any age would follow his way. They too would often be considered to be of the devil, though it would not always be expressed in that way.

But how could this be? Jesus taught about God, healed disease, told magnificent truths in stories. But what we can so easily miss is that the news that is good for one may be heard by another as a very great threat. We can see this in the Old Testament. A prophet like Amos would come and ask very uncomfortable questions. Why were so many people poor? Why could so many officials be easily bribed? The truth was being spoken but it brought sharply different reactions.

So it was with Our Lord. To us a story such as that of the Samaritan seems harmless. However if we had heard it as a Jew of Jesus' time we would realize that we and our church and our society were being sharply criticized for our neglect of many needs. We would probably be extremely angry and express that anger. We might try to find ways to deny what we had heard. We might say defensively that a rural rabbi has no idea how complex social issues are, or that perhaps this fellow is nothing less than disloyal and subversive and should be legally dealt with, perhaps even done away with!

So it was and so it will always be. Helder Camara, the physically tiny and now elderly Archbishop of Recife in Brazil, is recognized by many as a giant of compassion and courage. He once said ''When I gave the poor bread they said I was a saint. When I asked why the poor were hungry they said I was a Marxist.'' When Our Lord hears this he must find it very familiar. It was his own experience, and it is the experience of many Christians today. The courage with which they face such experiences is our Good News for this week.

Sunday between 26 June and 2 July

[34]"Do not think that I have come to bring peace on earth; I have not come to bring peace, but a sword. [35]For I have come to set a man against his father, and a daughter against her mother, and a daughter-in-law against her mother-in-law; [36]and a man's foes will be those of his own household. [37]He who loves father or mother more than me is not worthy of me; and he who loves son or daughter more than me is not worthy of me; [38]and he who does not take his cross and follow me is not worthy of me. [39]He who finds his life will lose it, and he who loses his life for my sake will find it. [40]"He who receives you receives me, and he who receives me receives him who sent me. [41]He who receives a prophet because he is a prophet shall receive a prophet's reward, and he who receives a righteous man because he is a righteous man shall receive a righteous man's reward. [42]And whoever gives to one of these little ones even a cup of cold water because he is a disciple, truly, I say to you, he shall not lose his reward."

Matthew 10:34–42

As we make real commitments to our human relationships, so Our Lord demands our commitment to him.

When we mingle religious faith with the power of family relationships we have a very powerful mixture. Let's take an example. A parent or both parents may have a passionate commitment to Christian faith. The very strength of this commitment may lead them into the trap of trying to superimpose this faith on a teenaged son or daughter. Their efforts may be totally self-defeating: intimacy can turn into alienation. A family can learn something of the truth in Jesus' statement that "a man's foes will be those of his own household."

When religion becomes an issue in a family the most important task is to do everything possible to keep the relationship from breaking. But how does this square with what Our Lord says next [v 37]? He tells us that we must love him more than those who are dearest to us.

At the risk of seeming to wriggle away from a radical demand of Our Lord, we need to realize that he was very much a man of his own eastern culture. He would sometimes emphasize a demand by exaggerating it. For instance, he suggests on another occasion that we should cut off a limb if it offends.

Our Lord is asking that the quality of our love for him be at very least of the same depth and intensity as the quality of our love and commitment for those dearest to us. We will make sacrifices for them. Will we make sacrifices for him? We will give time to them. Will we give time to him? We will give our utmost to strengthening and nourishing relationships with them. Will we do at least the same for our relationship with him? Just as we are the only ones who can make these decisions about our human relationships, so only we can decide about the quality of our relationship with Our Lord.

There is so much profound content in this passage we can touch only some of it. In verse 38 and verse 39 Our Lord says two things that have echoed down the centuries. In asking us that we take up our cross he is demanding that we take responsibility for our allegiance to him. Is that allegiance real? Each of us must answer that. In verse 39 Jesus tells us of a paradox at the heart of life. The more we try to possess life for self-centred ends the more we lose its essential meaning and joy. The more we give ourselves to Our Lord the more real we will find ourselves to be. Finally in verse 42 Our Lord once again implies that the ultimate measuring rod for our Christian faith is our actions. Loving him is not a sentimental concept. Love is obedience to him. Love is a deed done for another. That is the Good News of this week.

Sunday between 3 and 9 July

²⁵At that time Jesus declared, ''I thank thee, Father, Lord of heaven and earth, that thou hast hidden these things from the wise and understanding and revealed them to babes; ²⁶yea, Father, for such was thy gracious will. ²⁷All things have been delivered to me by my Father; and no one knows the Son except the Father, and no one knows the Father except the Son and any one to whom the Son chooses to reveal him. ²⁸Come to me, all who labor and are heavy laden, and I will give you rest. ²⁹Take my yoke upon you, and learn from me; for I am gentle and lowly in heart, and you will find rest for your souls. ³⁰For my yoke is easy, and my burden is light.''

Matthew 11:25–30

Our Lord's invitation to us is to look to him, then to follow his way in the world of our time.

In this passage we hear Jesus voicing a frequent theme. Our Lord wants us to understand something contradictory and often puzzling, something about the way God and our lives can be in contact. He says that to keep such lines of contact open we must be as children, and he actually took a child on his knee to emphasize it. That does not mean being childish; it means being childlike, which is very different. What is the essence of childhood which diminishes with adulthood? It is trust, that ability to trust in oneself, in other people, and in God. It is also the capacity to love unconditionally. Thirdly, it is the feeling that anything is possible. Frogs can become princes, people can change. On the other hand, it is the capacity to take people exactly as they are. All such things are of the kingdom of God yet they don't exist easily in the kingdom of everyday adult life! They are considered naive and unrealistic, yet Our Lord calls us to nourish and treasure them.

In verse 27 Our Lord tries to show us that between him and his father there is a deep and intimate relationship. Jesus then suggests that, if we wish to see a portrait of the nature of God, we look at Jesus himself.

That statement is deep and mystical and it can speak to us about all our human relationships. There are people around us through whom we can catch glimpses of God, people in whose lives and actions and attitudes we come in contact with the same love and grace which were found by those who came in contact with Jesus. We also need to remember that this same love and grace can be found in those around us who may not acknowledge Jesus as their Lord. It is very easy to forget that.

In verse 28 Our Lord says something so beautiful and appealing it has never been forgotten. It is his invitation to follow him and his way. He lets us know that he fully realizes the struggle that human life can be, the restlessness of it all, the challenge and the drain it can be. He then offers himself and his way to us as a resource for living our lives. His way is not complicated. It is not a long list of thou-shalt-nots. It is a simple deciding that we will accept him into our lives as Lord. All the Christian generations have used many other words to describe a relationship with Our Lord. St Richard in England called him ''Redeemer, Friend, Brother.'' Other images such as Master, Guide, Comforter may speak to us. The image is not important; the relationship we have is all-important. That is the Good News for this week.

Sunday between 10 and 16 July

[1]That same day Jesus went out of the house and sat beside the sea. [2]And great crowds gathered about him, so that he got into a boat and sat there; and the whole crowd stood on the beach. [3]And he told them many things in parables, saying: ''A sower went out to sow. [4]And as he sowed, some seeds fell along the path, and the birds came and devoured them. [5]Other seeds fell on rocky ground, where they had not much soil, and immediately they sprang up, since they had no depth of soil, [6]but when the sun rose they were scorched; and since they had no root they withered away. [7]Other seeds fell upon thorns, and the thorns grew up and choked them. [8]Other seeds fell on good soil and brought forth grain, some a hundredfold, some sixty, some thirty. [9]He who has ears, let him hear.''

[18]''Hear then the parable of the sower. [19]When any one hears the word of the kingdom and does not understand it, the evil one comes and snatches away what is sown in his heart; this is what was sown along the path. [20]As for what was sown on rocky ground, this is he who hears the word and immediately receives it with joy; [21] yet he has no root in himself, but endures for a while, and when tribulation or persecution arises on account of the word, immediately he falls away. [22]As for what was sown among thorns, this is he who hears the word, but the cares of the world and the delight in riches choke the word, and it proves unfruitful. [23]As for what was sown on good soil, this is he who hears the word and understands it; he indeed bears fruit, and yields, in one case a hundredfold, in another sixty, and in another thirty.''

Matthew 13:1–9, 18–23

God sows the seed. We are the ground which receives it. What kind of ground do we decide to be?

There are all sorts of ways by which we come to faith. One person cannot point to a moment when Jesus became their Lord because they have never known a period when Jesus was not part of their consciousness. Someone else may have had a totally different experience. Through some event, some book, some relationship, some conversation, they may have been brought to deciding that Jesus was their Lord. The sad thing is that sometimes the latter person will think the former person's way to be not quite the real thing. Of course it is the real thing. It may be gradual, even lifelong, but it can be profoundly real.

Jesus told a story about the many kinds of faith journeys people experience. His image of God is that of a sower striding along a stretch of ground. In long regular sweeps of his arm he throws the seed far and wide. That seed represents all the myriad ways in which God communicates with us and gives grace to us.

A seed falls on the roadway beyond the soil line. A bird comes and the seed is gone. A seed falls among rocks where there is just a sprinkling of earth. It grows but it has no nourishment, so it dies. A seed falls among thorns, struggles to grow, succeeds partially, and is overcome. Finally a seed falls in good rich earth and there are magnificent results.

In a sense the whole story is true of each of our lives. From birth to death God communicates with us, fostering our growth, guiding, inspiring, calling. Because we are human we go through periods and circumstances when we become each of those places in the story where the seed of God tries to grow. We can be the path beyond the soil line. That may be a stage in our lives when other influences, some of them actually evil, can snatch from us any link with Our Lord. We can become the rocky ground, a person full of initial enthusiasm, but if there comes a time when our allegiance to Our Lord becomes costly in any way, we fade out. We can be the place of thorns. We encounter Our Lord. It affects us deeply, but something more attractive comes and we go in that direction. There are a host of shiny options in today's world to make us do just that. Finally we can become good soil. We encounter Our Lord. We grow in him and we respond to Him. He becomes the foundation of our lives. We find that life with him can be far more satisfying than the other shiny options. That's the Good News for this week.

Sunday between 17 and 23 July

²⁴Another parable he put before them, saying, ''The kingdom of heaven may be compared to a man who sowed good seed in his field; ²⁵but while men were sleeping, his enemy came and sowed weeds among the wheat, and went away. ²⁶So when the plants came up and bore grain, then the weeds appeared also. ²⁷And the servants of the householder came and said to him, 'Sir, did you not sow good seed in your field? How then has it weeds?' ²⁸He said to them, 'An enemy has done this.' The servants said to him. 'Then do you want us to go and gather them?' ²⁹But he said, 'No; lest in gathering the weeds you root up the wheat along with them. ³⁰Let both grow together until the harvest; and at harvest time I will tell the reapers, Gather the weeds first and bind them in bundles to be burned, but gather the wheat into my barn.' ''

³⁶Then he left the crowds and went into the house. And his disciples came to him, saying, ''Explain to us the parable of the weeds of the field.'' ³⁷He answered, ''He who sows the good seed is the Son of man; ³⁸the field is the world, and the good seed means the sons of the kingdom; the weeds are the sons of the evil one, ³⁹and the enemy who sowed them is the devil; the harvest is the close of the age, and the reapers are angels. ⁴⁰Just as the weeds are gathered and burned with fire, so will it be at the close of the age. ⁴¹The Son of man will send his angels, and they will gather out of his kingdom all causes of sin and all evildoers, ⁴²and throw them into the furnace of fire; there men will weep and gnash their teeth. ⁴³Then the righteous will shine like the sun in the kingdom of their Father. He who has ears, let him hear.''

Matthew 13:24–30, 36–43

Life and history will always be a mingling of good and evil, light and darkness. Even our best efforts will not attain perfection.

Human life is constantly caught between things as they are and things as we would wish them to be, or as we can imagine they could be. We can imagine a perfect relationship but we cannot have one. We can imagine a world of perfect peace and justice but we can never succeed in building one. Our best efforts fall very far short of perfection. We live in the great gulf between the actual and the possible.

Our Lord knows that very well. The central fact of Christian faith is that he came to live in that gulf. He once expressed his thoughts about it all in a story in which he was really talking about the rule or kingdom of God.

A man sowed good seed in a field. Overnight someone sowed weeds. When the field grew there was this ghastly mixture. The farm hands were appalled. They offered to clean up the field. The owner told them not to because they would damage the crop itself. He tells them to wait till harvest, then the weeds and the wheat will be separated and their true values shown.

Later on [v 37] Jesus explains the story to his disciples. The world is made up of good and evil elements. There will come a day when there will be a reckoning. Our Lord points to a relentless judgement. Human life is accountable and must be lived in the certain knowledge of that accounting. But notice the implication behind the fact that this accounting does not take place until ''the close of the age.'' In Our Lord's story this is expressed by the farmer's telling his reapers that they are not to separate wheat and weeds now but to wait until the ''harvest.'' What is this waiting until the harvest or the close of the age?

Our Lord seems to be telling us something that is inevitable in human experience. Everything about human existence is ambiguous, whether in our own lives or the life of the community or of the whole society. Every aspect of existence has an essentially tragic element within it. It is always mingled light and dark, good and evil, positive and negative. Our Lord is pointing out that this will be so until the end of time. We cannot bring into being a perfect person. We cannot form the perfect community or the perfect society or church or culture or civilization. This does not mean that we do not work to reform what we consider evil in human existence. But we can have no illusion that perfection is attainable. Final judgement is simply not ours; it rests with the Lord of history. But that judgement is utterly certain. That is the Good News for this week.

Sunday between 24 and 30 July

44"The kingdom of heaven is like treasure hidden in a field, which a man found and covered up; then in his joy he goes and sells all that he has and buys that field. 45"Again, the kingdom of heaven is like a merchant in search of fine pearls, 46who, on finding one pearl of great value, went and sold all that he had and bought it. 47"Again, the kingdom of heaven is like a net which was thrown into the sea and gathered fish of every kind; 48when it was full, men drew it ashore and sat down and sorted the good into vessels but threw away the bad. 49So it will be at the close of the age. The angels will come out and separate the evil from the righteous, 50and throw them into the furnace of fire; there men will weep and gnash their teeth. 51"Have you understood all this?" They said to him, "Yes." 52And he said to them, "Therefore every scribe who has been trained for the kingdom of heaven is like a householder who brings out of his treasure what is new and what is old."

Matthew 13:44–52

If the kingdom of God could make all the difference to life, how much would we be prepared to give for it?

Everyone knows the feeling of wanting something so much that you would give everything you have to possess it. Very often we experience that feeling in childhood. It is by no means absent in adulthood, but we are less likely to accept the terms of such a transaction. However, we often accept a trade-off without realizing it. Many a man or woman has sacrificed everything else in life for the rewards of professional success, only to find that the prize was not worth the sacrifice.

Whenever Jesus begins any statement with the words "the kingdom of heaven" we know that he is trying to express what human life would be like if our thinking and acting reflected completely God's will for us. In this case Jesus shows us a man finding treasure in a field. The man immediately hides it again, sells everything he has, and buys the field.

The treasure in the field is our relationship with God. Our Lord is suggesting that this is the ultimate great prize in life. How much value are we prepared to put on such a possession? How much are we prepared to pay?

At first glance Jesus' second story seems the same but it is very different. In fact to realize the difference is to be deeply moved. In this story the merchant looking for fine pearls is actually God [known to us in Jesus as Our Lord] who is in search of us. And when he finds one of us he is prepared to give everything, even life itself, for us. We might take a moment to reflect on the immense value and worth this accords to us, a worth far beyond what we expect or deserve. To realize who the merchant in this parable really is, is to realize the great love by which we are loved. Once again we are faced with a decision. What response are we prepared to make to this love?

We hear a third story [v 47]. A net splashes into the lake. It emerges full of fish; some are thrown back into the water. They have been judged unworthy of use. So it will be in life, Jesus tells us. Once again Our Lord is returning to a theme he hammers home again and again. Human life is lived in full freedom to make its moral choices. But that freedom carries a price. To be free is to be answerable for one's choices; this gives life its essential meaning. That is the Good News for this week.

Sunday between 31 July and 6 August

¹³Now when Jesus heard this, he withdrew from there in a boat to a lonely place apart. But when the crowds heard it, they followed him on foot from the towns. ¹⁴As he went ashore he saw a great throng; and he had compassion on them, and healed their sick. ¹⁵When it was evening, the disciples came to him and said, "This is a lonely place, and the day is now over; send the crowds away to go into the villages and buy food for themselves." ¹⁶Jesus said, "They need not go away; you give them something to eat." ¹⁷They said to him, "We have only five loaves here and two fish." ¹⁸And he said, "Bring them here to me." ¹⁹Then he ordered the crowds to sit down on the grass; and taking the five loaves and the two fish he looked up to heaven, and blessed, and broke and gave the loaves to the disciples, and the disciples gave them to the crowds. ²⁰And they all ate and were satisfied. And they took up twelve baskets full of the broken pieces left over. ²¹And those who ate were about five thousand men, besides women and children.

Matthew 14:13–21

We are called in life to serve God with the resources we have at hand, using them in God's service and thus finding them blessed.

What does one do when one has heard ghastly news? Sometimes one tries desperately to be alone. We meet Jesus at such a moment. He has just heard that his friend John, the person at whose hands he had received baptism, has been brutally murdered. As is often the case Jesus finds it impossible to find solitude. Crowds follow him. Notice Our Lord's response to this. There is no display of anger, no resentment, no claiming his right to solitude. Instead there is much caring for these people. When someone suggests that the crowd should disperse to the local communities for food Jesus instead assumes responsibility for their welfare. Using some materials at hand he feeds them.

The story teaches a great deal about the human situation. Take, for instance, Our Lord's response to his being followed. He needed and wanted to be alone. He had every right to be. Yet, as we see, there is no pushing away; there is total acceptance. So often in life we would serve ourselves and those around us better by *accepting* certain situations, seeing what we can do with what has been given to us.

The instinct of the disciples is to get rid of the crowds, to shift responsibility. In the circumstances it seems very reasonable. But Our Lord wants to teach a truth: whenever possible we are called to accept responsibility.

The disciples are realists. There simply is not enough available to do the job. But sometimes there needs to be someone who is prepared to risk challenging what seems to be realistic. There are countless moments in history when realism pointed the way to a certain course of action, but history was changed because someone refused the arguments of realism and chose to go another way. This is such a moment.

The fact that Our Lord takes the pitiable supply of resources, a little bread and fish, is itself a lesson. He seems to be saying to us that he is prepared to use the poor and limited resources which we have to offer for his use. God is willing to use us. We are in a sense the bread and the fish with which Our Lord is prepared to feed the world. All this depends of course on our being available for his use.

Notice that Our Lord blesses the resources and thereby they become more than they originally were. The same is true of each one of us. With Our Lord's grace we are capable of being transformed. With his love we are capable of a greater love. With his spirit augmenting our spirit we can be greater instruments of his will than we have ever dreamed. That is the Good News for this week.

Sunday between 7 and 13 August

²²Then he made the disciples get into the boat and go before him to the other side, while he dismissed the crowds. ²³And after he had dismissed the crowds, he went up on the mountain by himself to pray. When evening came, he was there alone. ²⁴But the boat by this time was many furlongs distant from the land, beaten by the waves; for the wind was against them. ²⁵And in the fourth watch of the night he came to them, walking on the sea. ²⁶But when the disciples saw him walking on the sea, they were terrified, saying, "It is a ghost!" And they cried out for fear. ²⁷But immediately he spoke to them, saying, "Take heart, it is I; have no fear." ²⁸And Peter answered him, "Lord, if it is you, bid me come to you on the water." ²⁹He said, "Come." So Peter got out of the boat and walked on the water and came to Jesus; ³⁰but when he saw the wind, he was afraid, and beginning to sink he cried out, "Lord, save me." ³¹Jesus immediately reached out his hand and caught him, saying to him, "O man of little faith, why did you doubt?" ³²And when they got into the boat, the wind ceased. ³³And those in the boat worshiped him, saying, "Truly you are the Son of God."

Matthew 14:22–33

In the storms of life Our Lord can bear us up.

Like any inland stretch of water, especially one surrounded by hills, the lake of Galilee can be transformed in a few minutes from calm to storm; it is full of unexpected changes and challenges. This same lake is so much at the heart of the gospel events that we can come to see it and the things that happened on it as representing events and patterns in our own lives. The lake, if you will, is human life itself, the journeys taken across it are our journeys, the struggles on it our struggles.

Here in this passage we share a moment in the turbulent relationship between Our Lord and the disciples. The crowd has been fed. Jesus sends the disciples over to the far side of the lake, promising to follow. He stays to see the people off. By the time they are gone night has fallen. Out on the lake things have turned ugly; a wind has made the water very dangerous and the boat is in considerable difficulty. The fact that it is pitch dark makes the situation even worse. At this point Our Lord appears to them, moving over the waters. They are terrified. Typically the one who responds is Peter. Impelled by the sight of his Master he leaves the boat, reaching for Jesus. Suddenly his courage fails him and he goes under. Our Lord reaches for him and rescues him.

What is being said to us? First we all have to take our voyage across the lake because the lake is life itself. We all take that voyage in the fearful and vulnerable vessel called the self. Because of the vulnerability we frequently travel with other selves. To each of us there comes a time of storm, of struggle, and fear. In such a time we feel it to be night in our lives. It is in fact at night that we do a great part of our wrestling with those thoughts that storm the defences of our half-asleep mind.

At such times Our Lord can and does come to us ''in the fourth watch of the night.'' In our fear he will say in many ways to us, ''Take heart, it is I; have no fear.'' We will indeed take heart in the face of what is troubling us. We will make our decision to resist fear. Like Peter we will get up and risk ourselves to the storm within us, trying to conquer our fear. Sometimes in such a situation we can falter as Peter did. The storm howls around us. The world seems to give way beneath us; we begin to sink. At such a moment

Our Lord can and does reach out to us. There can be new strength and stability. There can be a stilling of the inner storm. This has been true for many who have trusted him, and it can be true for us. That is the Good News for this week.

Sunday between 14 and 20 August

21And Jesus went away from there and withdrew to the district of Tyre and Sidon. 22And behold, a Canaanite woman from that region came out and cried, "Have mercy on me, O Lord, Son of David; my daughter is severely possessed by a demon." 23But he did not answer her a word. And his disciples came and begged him, saying, "Send her away, for she is crying after us." 24He answered, "I was sent only to the lost sheep of the house of Israel." 25But she came and knelt before him, saying, "Lord, help me." 26And he answered, "It is not fair to take the children's bread and throw it to the dogs." 27She said, "Yes, Lord, yet even the dogs eat the crumbs that fall from their masters' table." 28Then Jesus answered her, "O woman, great is your faith! Be it done for you as you desire." And her daughter was healed instantly.

Matthew 15:21–28

Sometimes God may use someone or some circumstances in our lives to force us to grow towards what he intends us to be.

Perhaps at some time someone forced us to do some painful growing. Probably at the time we didn't appreciate it, but afterwards we realized they were pushing us precisely because they knew we were capable of being more than we ourselves realized.

That happens to Jesus in this passage. He is travelling outside his own country. A woman comes to him with a request. An approach like hers is perfectly familiar to him but this particular encounter is to be different.

Jesus has withdrawn because he wishes to detach himself for a while from the unrelenting demands of the public role he had chosen. When the woman turns up, the fact that she deliberately calls him ''Son of David'' signals to him that she has heard of him and of his healing gifts. Her request is that Jesus heal her child.

Notice how very humanly Jesus reacts. In his tiredness and wish to escape he simply does not respond at all [v 23]. That should come to us as assurance that Our Lord understands and forgives our own times of failing to respond to this or that demand because we are simply worn out.

The disciples try once again to get rid of her, but the woman asks again. This time Jesus actually refuses her. He seems to feel that his public role is possible only within his own country and people. He is limiting himself. What we are seeing very clearly is the humanity of Jesus. Far from disappointing us it should assure us of the genuineness of his humanity.

But the woman does not give up. Once again she asks. Once again she is refused by Jesus, this time hurtfully [v 26]. The reply she gets draws a very definite circle and shuts her out. But once again this courageous woman approaches. She takes Jesus' hurtful image of throwing crumbs to dogs and shows him that for the love of her child and because of her trust in him she is prepared to beg if that is necessary [v 27]. It is this that breaks through Jesus' resistance. Amazed by the sheer magnificence of this woman, he grants her request.

What we have seen is a person forcing the humanity of Jesus to realize that he is called to be what he really is, a spiritual resource for the world. What the episode says to us is that we may need to do a great deal of growing to become what God intends us to be. We need to be open to those with whom we come in contact who may force us, even if we do not want to, to grow. That is the Good News for this week.

Sunday between 21 and 27 August

¹³Now when Jesus came into the district of Caesarea
Philippi, he asked his disciples, "Who do men say that
the Son of man is?" ¹⁴And they said, "Some say John
the Baptist, others say Elijah, and others Jeremiah or
one of the prophets." ¹⁵He said to them, "But who
do you say that I am?" ¹⁶Simon Peter replied, "You
are the Christ, the Son of the living God." ¹⁷And Jesus
answered him, "Blessed are you, Simon Bar-Jona! For
flesh and blood has not revealed this to you, but my
Father who is in heaven. ¹⁸And I tell you, you are
Peter, and on this rock I will build my church, and the
powers of death shall not prevail against it. ¹⁹I will
give you the keys of the kingdom of heaven, and
whatever you bind on earth shall be bound in heaven,
and whatever you loose on earth shall be loosed in
heaven." ²⁰Then he strictly charged the disciples to
tell no one that he was the Christ.

Matthew 16:13–20

**Our Lord asks every one of us, "Who do you say that I
am?"**

Caesarea Philippi was a beautiful, dangerous, and tough
locality. Today its ruins are on the edge of a national park
in Northern Galilee. In those days it was a rest and recreation centre for the Roman army. The city was dedicated to
the god Pan, probably the most sensual of the gods.

It was in this city, surrounded by a seamy and very secular society, that Jesus decided to ask his disciples a key question [v 13]. He asked them, "Who do men say the Son of
man is?" But perhaps the next question Jesus asked is more
important. After he had listened to their various replies he
said, "Who do you say that I am?"

That question placed everyone on the spot. Peter blurted out that Jesus was the Christ. That moment stays totally alive through time. Our Lord asks this question of us now and asks it in exactly the same words, ''Who do you say I am?''

Each one of us alone knows the reply we have tried to make up to now in our lives. Maybe we have already said to Our Lord, as Peter said, ''You are the Christ.'' If we haven't we have got to say it at some stage if our relationship with him is to be strong and lasting.

We said that Caesarea Philippi was dangerous and beautiful, sexual and secular. It's interesting that Our Lord chose that place to ask his question. Look at the world we live in, the world where we are trying to be his disciples. Can that urban world of ours not be seen in very much the same terms as Caesarea Philippi? It certainly can be tough and dangerous; in places it can be extremely beautiful and impressive. It is also immensely intrigued by sexuality. Heaven knows it uses it endlessly, much of the time to sell us things we desire.

The point is that it is right in the middle of this very secular world that Our Lord ask us his eternal question. He demands that we state our allegiance to him. Notice what he says to Peter after Peter's expression of faith. Jesus defined that faith as the rock on which Christian community can be built. Likewise our faith, if it is real, becomes a rich and strong base on which God's work in the Christian community can be founded. Our Lord depends on us. That is the Good News for this week.

Sunday between 28 August and 3 September

²¹From that time Jesus began to show his disciples that he must go to Jerusalem and suffer many things from the elders and chief priests and scribes, and be killed, and on the third day be raised. ²²And Peter took him and began to rebuke him, saying, ''God forbid, Lord! This shall never happen to you.'' ²³But he turned and said to Peter, ''Get behind me, Satan! You are a hindrance to me; for you are not on the side of God, but of men.'' ²⁴Then Jesus told his disciples, ''If any man would come after me, let him deny himself and take up his cross and follow me. ²⁵For whoever would save his life will lose it, and whoever loses his life for my sake will find it. ²⁶For what will it profit a man, if he gains the whole world and forfeits his life? Or what shall a man give in return for his life? ²⁷For the Son of man is to come with his angels in the glory of his Father, and then he will repay every man for what he has done. ²⁸Truly, I say to you, there are some standing here who will not taste death before they see the Son of man coming in his kingdom.''

Matthew 16:21–28

Winning and losing can have meanings very different from what we usually think if only we judge life by Our Lord's terms.

There is always a great deal we don't really want to hear, and we often go to great lengths to make sure that we don't. We practice what is called ''denial.'' Peter does this in this passage. He refuses to hear something supremely important that Jesus is trying to communicate. His refusal is so obvious that it triggers one of the sternest responses we hear from Our Lord in the whole Gospel narrative.

Our Lord knew by this time of the shadow that loomed over him. If he stayed in conflict with the religious and political powers of his day he would be destroyed, yet he was convinced there was no other way to accomplish his mission. This is what he tries to tell his disciples [v 21]. They obviously refuse to hear this, and Peter blatantly denies it. Our Lord is appalled, and expressing his anger and frustration, curtly dismisses Peter [v 23].

Jesus is so concerned by this denial from those nearest to him, that he speaks of the necessity for each of us to take up a cross [v 24]. What does that mean for us? Well, it will have many levels of meaning. We need not limit it to suffering only. Our Lord is also asking us to begin to commit ourselves wholeheartedly to him, and to assume full responsibility for our faith and for our faith journey through life.

Jesus then says something which has haunted humanity ever since. He says, ''Whoever would save his life will lose it, and whoever loses his life for my sake will find it.'' What could the first clause mean for our lives? Could it mean at one level that the more we cling on to things in life the more they slip through our fingers? Could it mean that the more we are determined to guard, defend, order, organize, and plan life, the more the very thing we are chasing will escape us? What we may be trying to grasp is ultimate security, cast-iron guarantees, and we cannot have them because life is just not like that.

''Whoever loses his life for my sake will find it.'' Is Our Lord saying that the more we can live the quality of his life, the more we will capture real life? What are those qualities? Utter trust in God, utter selflessness towards others. These are daunting demands, but when anyone has tried to reach for them, that person has discovered pearls beyond price. They haven't *lost* anything; instead they *find* something. That is the Good News for this week.

Sunday between 4 and 10 September

¹⁵"If your brother sins against you, go and tell him his fault, between you and him alone. If he listens to you, you have gained your brother. ¹⁶But if he does not listen, take one or two others along with you, that every word may be confirmed by the evidence of two or three witnesses. ¹⁷If he refuses to listen to them, tell it to the church; and if he refuses to listen even to the church, let him be to you as a Gentile and a tax collector. ¹⁸Truly, I say to you, whatever you bind on earth shall be bound in heaven, and whatever you loose on earth shall be loosed in heaven. ¹⁹Again I say to you, if two of you agree on earth about anything they ask, it will be done for them by my Father in heaven. ²⁰For where two or three are gathered in my name, there am I in the midst of them."

Matthew 18:15–20

How are disagreements and hurts to be dealt with in the Christian community?

We human beings can hurt each other very much. Sometimes we mean to and other times we are totally unaware. However, we rarely apply the benefit of that doubt to someone who has hurt us.

But when we are hurt or betrayed, how do we deal with it? The first thing most of us do is to lick the wound. Sometimes if we are of a certain temperament we take the risk of licking becoming a little enjoyable. We may also accept the hurt as satisfying proof that the person who hurt us is hateful and we can now indulge our dislike with full justification!

Jesus suggests that if somebody wrongs or hurts us we should make every effort to deal with it at the first opportunity, and, if at all possible, one on one. Jesus is being very realistic however. He knows that one on one may not work [v 16]. It may be necessary to bring in someone to check what was heard and said. Jesus goes further. If the disagreement between two people is within a Christian community, it may be possible to get together a small group of people whom both sides trust. Even then an utterly realistic Jesus sees the possibility of failure [v 17]. It simply may not be possible for the opponents to come to terms with each other. By saying this Our Lord is not saying that some future opportunity may not come to break through resistance.

Notice an interesting detail in Our Lord's advice. He says, "Let him [the person who has sinned against you] be to you as a Gentile and tax collector" [v 17]. There is an aspect of that statement that could be very useful in today's church. The attitude towards Gentiles and tax collectors in Jesus' society was a finely balanced one. There was a limit to the degree of relationship that was possible. In the case of tax collectors there was real dislike of them. But in both cases, and this is the point, there was much practical collaboration. Many things were done together in spite of the mutual guardedness. Likewise in today's church it is possible to do a great deal for Our Lord's work while serving side by side with those whom we may not particularly like, by whom, in fact, we may even have been hurt. True, it may not be easy. But if it can be done it can achieve miracles of reconciliation by sharing in a worthwhile task, knowing that in spite of human feelings about one another both are involved in the work of the same Lord. Is it being unrealistic to think this is possible? If so it is amazing how often the vision of Our Lord challenges our ideas of what is realistic. That is the Good News for this week.

Sunday between 11 and 17 September

²¹Then Peter came up and said to him, ''Lord, how often shall my brother sin against me, and I forgive him? As many as seven times?'' ²²Jesus said to him, ''I do not say to you seven times, but seventy times seven. ²³Therefore the kingdom of heaven may be compared to a king who wished to settle accounts with his servants. ²⁴When he began the reckoning, one was brought to him who owed him ten thousand talents; ²⁵and as he could not pay, his lord ordered him to be sold, with his wife and children and all that he had, and payment to be made. ²⁶So the servant fell on his knees, imploring him, 'Lord, have patience with me, and I will pay you everything.' ²⁷And out of pity for him the lord of that servant released him and forgave him the debt. ²⁸But that same servant, as he went out, came upon one of his fellow servants who owed him a hundred denarii; and seizing him by the throat he said, 'Pay what you owe.' ²⁹So his fellow servant fell down and besought him, 'Have patience with me, and I will pay you.' ³⁰He refused and went and put him in prison till he should pay the debt. ³¹When his fellow servants saw what had taken place, they were greatly distressed, and they went and reported to their lord all that had taken place. ³²Then his lord summonded him and said to him, 'You wicked servant! I forgave you all that debt because you besought me; ³³and should not you have had mercy on your fellow servant, as I had mercy on you?' ³⁴And in anger his lord delivered him to the jailers, till he should pay all his debt. ³⁵So also my heavenly Father will do to every one of you, if you do not forgive your brother from your heart.''

Matthew 18:21–35

We cannot receive forgiveness unless we are prepared to give it.

All of us have problems with forgiveness. There are little things in life which are easy to forgive because they don't really test us, but all of us can experience deep hurts and betrayals which really do. I suspect that most of us know at least one person who carries the grim burden of not being able to forgive.

The subject came up one day between Jesus and his disciples. Jesus had just been chatting about the handling of hurts and disagreements, the ways to try to reopen communication between people. If we look back at the verse [v 20] just before this passage, we see Jesus saying that wherever two or three are gathered in his name he is there in their midst. Our Lord seems to be saying that when we succeed in finding reconciliation or oneness between us he is actually there!

It was Peter who responded to the theme of looking for reconciliation. He asked a very human question. How many times should one forgive? To answer his own question he suggests the standards he grew up with. The law suggested seven times; by human standards that is most gracious. But Jesus rather takes the wind out of our sails by demanding that we have no limit to our forgiving. In effect that is what "seventy times seven" means. To illustrate it Jesus tells the story of the man who, forgiven a large debt, went out and forced someone to pay him back an outstanding tiny debt. What Our Lord is teaching us is the devastating truth that we should be perpetually forgiving because we ourselves are perpetually in need of forgiveness by other people and most certainly by God!

Our Lord is trying to get us to understand that forgiving and being forgiven is a mysterious and complex process. The whole point of the story is that the man who refuses to forgive someone else cannot really accept and benefit from the forgiveness he himself has received in the first place.

When we ourselves are hurt or betrayed, how are we at forgiving? How high do we rate its importance? At first sight it doesn't seem too vital an ability; many others seem more important. (Very few professional questionnaires ask us to rate our capacity for forgiveness!) Yet forgiving is so important for Our Lord that he places it right at the heart of the prayer he taught us. That clause is also the only conditional one in the prayer; it says that we can receive forgiveness only if we give it. Nothing could be more understandable. That so many people have found it to be true in their lives is the Good News for this week.

Sunday between 18 and
24 September

20"For the kingdom of heaven is like a householder who went out early in the morning to hire laborers for his vineyard. ²After agreeing with the laborers for a denarius a day, he sent them into his vineyard. ³And going out about the third hour he saw others standing idle in the market place; ⁴and to them he said, 'You go into the vineyard too, and whatever is right I will give you.' So they went. ⁵Going out again about the sixth hour and the ninth hour, he did the same. ⁶And about the eleventh hour he went out and found others standing; and he said to them, 'Why do you stand here idle all day?' ⁷They said to him, 'Because no one has hired us.' He said to them, 'You go into the vineyard too.' ⁸And when evening came, the owner of the vineyard said to his steward, 'Call the laborers and pay them their wages, beginning with the last, up to the first.' ⁹And when those hired about the eleventh hour came, each of them received a denarius. ¹⁰Now when the first came, they thought they would receive more; but each of them also received a denarius. ¹¹And on receiving it they grumbled at the householder, ¹²saying, 'These last worked only one hour, and you have made them equal to us who have borne the burden of the day and the scorching heat.' ¹³But he replied to one of them, 'Friend, I am doing you no wrong; did you not agree with me for a denarius? ¹⁴Take what belongs to you, and go; I choose to give to this last as I give to you. ¹⁵Am I not allowed to do what I choose with what belongs to me? Or do you begrudge my generosity?' ¹⁶So the last will be first, and the first last.''

Matthew 20:1–16

The generosity of God is greater than human justice.

Once again Jesus is talking to us about the kingdom of heaven. When Jesus does this we know that he is trying to explain to us how the world would be if the rule of God were obeyed universally.

Our Lord is speaking to us about our concepts of justice and God's concepts. The scene Jesus paints would be familiar to anyone in Canada who knows the pick-up points for day labour on the farms or ranches around a city. Jesus tells of an estate owner who hires workers in the dawn hours. They agree on a penny or denarius, the official minimum wage for a day's work. The owner goes out again and again that day, so that the last to be hired have only an hour's work. However, when time comes to pay everyone all get the same amount, a denarius. Naturally there is grumbling about unfairness. The owner dismisses the charge, claiming to be free to do as he wants with his money.

Notice what the unfairness charge centres on. No one can say he was given less than he should have been given. The earliest made a contract, the others after that didn't, but they have got more than the minimum rate. What probably enrages everyone is that the last batch get a whole day's wages for one hour's work. Should not everyone have been paid proportionately to the amount of the day worked?

Of course that's right, we say. But Jesus' estate owner says no, not on his estate it isn't! Why? Because remember that this is a story about the kingdom of heaven, about God's ways, not our ways. Jesus is teaching that God's way is more generous than human justice. Human justice would have to be in minimal terms; the contract with the first workers would be the measure and all succeeding agreements would be calculated downwards. God's justice is that the first contract be the level to which all others are lifted.

In daily life what might this be about? Let's consider two people. One grows all his or her life in the knowledge of God and with faith, worshipping regularly. In that life God is a reality from which comes meaning and joy and purpose. The other person lives for many years without any thought of God. To that person faith is irrelevant, religion is for fools, Christ is merely an oath. Then for some reason everything changes for this person. Faith and God become living realities, Christ lives. There is purpose, new meaning, real joy, all now just as spiritually nourishing as in the first person's life. One person has served Christ for many years, the other has just discovered the service of Christ. That is God's way. God does not measure. God gives the Holy Spirit abundantly. That is the Good News for this week.

Sunday between 25 September and 1 October

28"What do you think? A man had two sons; and he went to the first and said, 'Son, go and work in the vineyard today,'29And he answered, 'I will not'; but afterward he repented and went. 30And he went to the second and said the same; and he answered, 'I go, sir,' but did not go. 31Which of the two did the will of his father?'' They said, ''The first.'' Jesus said to them, ''Truly, I say to you, the tax collectors and the harlots go into the kingdom of God before you. 32For John came to you in the way of righteousness, and you did not believe him, but the tax collectors and the harlots believed him; and even when you saw it, you did not afterward repent and believe him.

Matthew 21:28–32

If we knew the people of whom God thinks highly, we would get some real surprises!

Again and again Our Lord talks about obedience. He had a strong aversion to responses to himself which were long on words and short on action! He saw love very much in terms of obedience.

Two sons are asked to do something. One promises to do it but fails to produce. The other refuses at first but afterwards changes his mind and does it. The question Jesus puts to people around him is that of obedience. Who obeyed the father? The one who said an immediate "yes" and then walked away, or the one who said a stubborn "no" but returned to do the job?

Does this story remind us of another story Our Lord told, again about two sons? One disappears over the hill with his inheritance, wastes it, turns for home, and is passionately welcomed. The other never asks for anything, stays faithful, but ends up angry, self-righteous, unloving. Each story is an echo of the other. But the further we look the more we see a consistent pattern in Jesus' attitude to certain people. In this passage [v 31] Jesus must have made listeners gasp when he said that prostitutes had a better chance of making it into God's kingdom than the respectable, God-fearing burghers gathered around him. Jesus goes one step further. He points out that when John the Baptist pleaded for changes in the country's lifestyle, he was listened to by these same prostitutes and tax collectors, people treated with contempt, once again by these respectable and God-fearing citizens.

What is the thread through all this? It was heard all too clearly by the established men and women of Jesus' day, and it was certainly one factor, if not the main factor, which placed him on a cross.

Our Lord saw that there is an irony at the heart of life. It is better somehow to have come through some battling with the self. It is better to have failed and to recover than never to have tasted failure. It is better to have sinned and be sorry than to have always enjoyed some ghastly bland innocence. There is a kind of false religion that is terrified of acknowledging this. Jesus was surrounded by that kind of religion and our own time is full of it. The first son in this short parable is far less real in Jesus' eyes than the second. The second at least has a will! He is a real person. His obedience is more difficult to get but it is far more worth getting. Thank God for the honesty and realism of Our Lord! That's the Good News for this week.

Sunday between 2 and 8 October

33"Hear another parable. There was a householder who planted a vineyard, and set a hedge around it, and dug a wine press in it, and built a tower, and let it out to tenants, and went into another country. 34When the season of fruit drew near, he sent his servants to the tenants, to get his fruit; 35and the tenants took his servants and beat one, killed another, and stoned another. 36Again he sent other servants, more than the first; and they did the same to them. 37Afterward he sent his son to them, saying, 'They will respect my son.' 38But when the tenants saw the son, they said to themselves, 'This is the heir; come, let us kill him and have his inheritance.' 39And they took him and cast him out of the vineyard, and killed him. 40When therefore the owner of the vineyard comes, what will he do to those tenants?" 41They said to him, "He will put those wretches to a miserable death, and let out the vineyard to other tenants who will give him the fruits in their seasons." 42Jesus said to them, "Have you never read in the scriptures: 'The very stone which the builders rejected has become the head of the corner, this was the Lord's doing, and it is marvelous in our eyes? 43Therefore I tell you, the kingdom of God will be taken away from you and given to a nation producing the fruits of it.''

Matthew 21: 33–43

We sometimes have to make tough choices about the kingdom God offers us and the kingdom we ourselves want.

Jesus offered a vision to the people of his own time. As our risen Lord he offers the same vision to us. The vision is of a kingdom, what he always calls the kingdom of heaven.

It is another way of living life, a kind of alternate universe. Jesus didn't just *talk* of that vision, he *was* the vision. He didn't just *speak* of the demands of that kingdom, he *did* them!

So why didn't it all work out in a wonderfully successful way? Why didn't everybody think that Jesus and his vision were just what the world needed? It's difficult to frame a simple answer to this but we can try.

In his Gospel John has two phrases which express the tragedy without necessarily explaining it. He says "The world knew Him not . . . his own people received Him not." Why? John later reports a statement of Jesus which seems to answer that question. Jesus says, "This is the judgement, that the light has come into the world, and men loved darkness rather than light" [John 3.19]. There it is in the starkest and simplest of words — the tragic heart of the human condition. The Bible's word for this condition, itself simple and stark, is *Sin*.

This is what this parable of Jesus is about. In it he tells his own destiny. Jesus had no illusions about the consequences of his words and actions. He knew the dark depths of the human nature which surrounded him.

The ironic contradiction in human behaviour and experience is to reject that which is utterly in our interest to accept [v 42]. Our judgement is deeply flawed, and our choices are apt to be terribly wrong.

The kingdom that Jesus offers us is not taken from us by some grudging God; we ourselves choose something else. But even as we paint that grim portrait of our human nature another face shines through it, that of Our Lord. The face is a promise that in him our humanity is also capable of a shining glory. Through Our Lord we can if we choose set foot from time to time in the very kingdom we refuse most of the time. That is the Good News for this week.

Sunday between 9 and 15 October

¹And again Jesus spoke to them in parables, saying, ²"The kingdom of heaven may be compared to a king who gave a marriage feast for his son, ³and sent his servants to call those who were invited to the marriage feast, but they would not come. ⁴Again he sent other servants, saying, 'Tell those who are invited, Behold, I have made ready my dinner, my oxen and my fat calves are killed, and everything is ready; come to the marriage feast.' ⁵But they made light of it and went off, one to his farm, another to his business, ⁶while the rest seized his servants, treated them shamefully, and killed them. ⁷The king was angry, and he sent his troops and destroyed those murderers and burned their city. ⁸Then he said to his servants, 'The wedding is ready, but those invited were not worthy. ⁹Go therefore to the thoroughfares, and invite to the marriage feast as many as you find.' ¹⁰And those servants went out into the streets and gathered all whom they found, both bad and good; so the wedding hall was filled with guests. ¹¹But when the king came in to look at the guests, he saw there a man who had no wedding garment; ¹²and he said to him, 'Friend, how did you get in here without a wedding garment?' And he was speechless. ¹³Then the king said to the attendants, 'Bind him hand and foot, and cast him into the outer darkness; there men will weep and gnash their teeth.' ¹⁴For many are called, but few are chosen."

Matthew 22:1–14

All through our lives God is inviting us to something more, a kingdom we would be wise to examine.

John Sandford has said that if you wish to see this parable of the wedding feast acted out in contemporary life you have only to sit in the waiting room of any counsellor. Nobody in the room wishes to be as they are. They have come to the conclusion that they need help to deal with some aspect of themselves and can no longer maintain the illusion of self-sufficiency.

Sandford goes on to point to another interpretation of this parable of the waiting room. Because such people have been unable to remain self-sufficient, and have been injured spiritually and have had to seek for help, they often can not only be healed but also can go on to find what Sandford calls ''springs of creative living.'' Other people, seemingly strong and well balanced all their lives, may never have such an experience.

This is the great spiritual truth in Jesus' story. All the people we see invited first to the feast seem to be in charge of their lives. They operate businesses, run farms, are organized. They are busy, so busy in fact that the king's [God's] invitation to the feast [the kingdom] to taste another kind of existence is turned down. The king then turns and invites people who have needs. Luke's version of this story is even more specific. The king invites the ''poor, the crippled, the blind, the lame,'' those who have no illusions about their ability to survive without help.

What of the man without a wedding garment [v 11]? In the east it was a custom for a lord to send a special robe with an invitation. To arrive without this was incredibly careless or ignorant. Jesus seems to be saying that if we take the spiritual area of our lives and treat it with carelessness then we will suffer severe consequences. That is extremely significant because the fact of the matter is that most of us in today's world do regard the spiritual as a kind of optional extra to life, something to be chosen as a kind of hobby by those who like it.

Once again we are hearing Our Lord's most constant theme. We accept an invitation to the kingdom which God has to offer only when we are ready to acknowledge a need in our lives. The wonderful fact is that our need for grace may well be that which in the end makes us stronger than we ever were, because our strength is now in Our Lord rather than in ourselves. That's the Good News for this week.

Sunday between 16 and 22 October

¹⁵Then the Pharisees went and took counsel how to entangle him in his talk. ¹⁶And they sent their disciples to him, along with the Herodians, saying, "Teacher, we know that you are true, and teach the way of God truthfully, and care for no man; for you do not regard the position of men. ¹⁷Tell us, then, what you think. Is it lawful to pay taxes to Caesar, or not?" ¹⁸But Jesus, aware of their malice, said, "Why put me to the test, you hypocrites? ¹⁹Show me the money for the tax." And they brought him a coin. ²⁰And Jesus said to them, "Whose likeness and inscription is this?" ²¹They said, "Caesar's." Then he said to them, "Render therefore to Caesar the things that are Caesar's, and to God the things that are God's." ²²When they heard it, they marveled; and they left him and went away.

Matthew 22:15–22

Each of us must respond to Jesus' statement about God and Caesar. All of us belong to God. How much do we give Caesar?

This is a nasty moment. In the language of our time, it's a set-up. Our Lord is in a public place. Around him is the usual mixture of people, some attracted to what he is teaching, others just curious. Mingling with the group are some of his enemies. He is too popular to attack openly so they try to trap him into saying something that can be used to show that he is subversive. It's a gambit as old as politics. With studied and wide-eyed innocence someone asks the dangerous question prefaced by a stream of treacherous flattery. "Is it lawful to pay taxes to Caesar or not?" There must have been a dead silence. Anyone with any intelligence in the crowd would know what was at stake. If the teacher said *yes* he would be making enemies at every level of Jewish life. If he said *no* he would challenge the Roman occupation.

Our Lord's answer has come down through time. It is the reply of a razor-sharp mind. He holds up the coin and says, "Render to Caesar the things that are Caesar's, and unto God the things that are God's." Twenty centuries roll away but the question and the reply remain. Why? Because the question and answer present men and women with an eternal equation which has to be worked out in human life.

We all live somewhere between the two poles expressed as Caesar and God. Each of us has to live in what we tend to call the real world, the world of nine to five. Whether it is really the real world is another story. Each of us has to decide what we give to the "Caesar" of our nine-to-five life. Do we give everything, all our time, all our energy? Do we make that part of our life an ultimate value; in a word, do we make it our God? Or do we acknowledge that only the Lord God is ultimate and that this God demands our allegiance, our integrity, our trust, our worship. That's the real question.

It is a matter of not looking at our lives as being divided into two worlds, the world of work and the world of worship, with God in the latter but not in the former. Thinking like that has long been the trap of our culture. God is the God of both worlds. Not until we realize this are we able to begin to work out the relationship between Caesar and God for our lives. Even then working out the balance of that equation is always difficult and there are no neat answers. The important thing is to realize that the equation must be continually worked at if we are to be responsible stewards of the one life we have. That is the Good News for this week.

Sunday between 23 and 29 October

34But when the Pharisees heard that he had silenced the Sadducees, they came together. 35And one of them, a lawyer, asked him a question, to test him. 36"Teacher, which is the great commandment in the law?" 37And he said to him, "You shall love the Lord your God with all your heart, and with all your soul, and with all your mind. 38This is the great and first commandment. 39And a second is like it, You shall love your neighbor as yourself. 40On these two commandments depend all the law and the prophets."

Matthew 22:34–40

Underlying all laws and sanctions is the primary law of love.

All of us have had the experience of listening to two people conversing and realizing that their views and assumptions are so totally different that they can never communicate with each other.

This passage allows us to eavesdrop on such a moment in Our Lord's ministry. By now, well into that short ministry, there is no scarcity of antagonists. Already Jesus' attitudes and statements have attracted not only attention, but also deep resentment. This resentment comes from the many established and entrenched elements which were all around Jesus and exist in every society. Even more dangerous for Jesus, we see [v 34] that two such groups, the Pharisees and the Sadducees, who were usually in disagreement, have come together to put pressure on him. While it is not quite true to say that these were two political parties, it will do to help us understand the situation.

As frequently happened, someone asked Jesus a question which was really a trap. This time it was which of all the commandments in the Law was the most important. As he always did Our Lord pierced through the deceit and hypocrisy of the question. There were thousands of commands in the Law. It was and still is a magnificent system which penetrates into every conceivable area of human life. Indeed, when we are tempted to hear dismissals of the Jewish Law in the New Testament, we should never forget that its very complexity was saying that every aspect of being alive is holy and God is involved in it. That is a most important spiritual insight and we are indebted to the Jewish Law for it.

However, as with everything in life, there is a *but*. The *but* is our humanity. The Law was becoming an end in itself rather than a means to help people live. Arguments were endless, the scoring of points the objective. Human life and human need were becoming engulfed by something originally designed to serve life. That is why Jesus goes to the heart of all law when he replies. For Our Lord the ultimate criterion by which all actions are judged is that of love. Notice that in loving our neighbour as ourselves we must realize that we do not always like ourselves nor approve of our own actions. Loving our neighbour is not necessarily being uncritical. Notice too that the basis of all human loving is possessing a love for God. Experience shows that without this latter, the former, loving one's neighbour, fades out. Without the element of love all law eventually becomes cold and sterile. Our Lord, as always, expressed the realities at the heart of life. That is the Good News for this week.

Sunday between 30 October and 5 November

¹Then said Jesus to the crowds and to his disciples, ²"The scribes and the Pharisees sit on Moses' seat; ³so practice and observe whatever they tell you, but not what they do; for they preach, but do not practice. ⁴They bind heavy burdens, hard to bear, and lay them on men's shoulders; but they themselves will not move them with their finger. ⁵They do all their deeds to be seen by men; for they make their phylacteries broad and their fringes long, ⁶and they love the place of honor at feasts and the best seats in the synagogues, ⁷and salutations in the market places, and being called rabbi by men. ⁸But you are not to be called rabbi, for you have one teacher, and you are all brethren. ⁹And call no man your father on earth, for you have one Father, who is in heaven. ¹⁰Neither be called masters, for you have one master, the Christ. ¹¹He who is greatest among you shall be your servant; ¹²whoever exalts himself will be humbled, and whoever humbles himself will be exalted."

Matthew 23:1–12

The whole point of possessing power and authority is to use it in the service of others.

On the last evening that Our Lord spent with his disciples he did something that amazed and shocked them. At a certain point in the evening he walked over to the entrance, took the water jar and the towel always left there to wash people's feet, came back, knelt down and washed all the feet around the table. The disciples were stunned: this was the task for the lowest servant, and here was their master and leader doing it.

Jesus was communicating the truth that life is about servanthood. He tells us that the greater the authority given to us the more it should be spent in service to others rather than in being served. He said this to James and John when they came looking for authority in the form of power and self-advancement. He says it again in this passage.

Jesus' first target is people who preach one thing and do another [v 3]. It is one of the many ways in which we seek to direct others, to have power and authority. The second target for Our Lord is the self-aggrandisement of those who seek public acknowledgement and social prominence, who love to be given the kind of respect which makes them feel superior [v 5]. Having shown these quick, vivid portraits of behaviour that would have been perfectly familiar to his listeners, and may have painfully described some of them, Jesus begins to define what he is getting at. In verse 8 and verse 10 he takes three very familiar images of authority, rabbi, father, master, and he warns against seeking that kind of authority. Jesus is not against such authority if it is sought for the sake of service. He is against it if it is sought for its own sake.

Then Our Lord centres on the theme so often expressed in his ministry. Not only did he express this theme, he also lived it day by day. The core of his message is in verse 11. "He who is greatest among you shall be your servant." Right from the start this was the pattern nearest to Our Lord's heart. He had learned the great servant songs of the prophet Isaiah. He had decided that servanthood was the highest calling a human being could follow. In saying this Our Lord was once again challenging what society assumes as a value and was placing before it a diametrically opposite value, that of servanthood. As with all images of the kingdom it challenges our deepest instincts. We don't really want servanthood; we want authority. Jesus did not say we could not have authority. He pointed out that we can have it if we exercise it in service. That is the Good News for this week.

Sunday between 6 and 12 November

[1]"Then the kingdom of heaven shall be compared to ten maidens who took their lamps and went to meet the bridegroom. [2]Five of them were foolish, and five were wise. [3]For when the foolish took their lamps, they took no oil with them; [4]but the wise took flasks of oil with their lamps. [5]As the bridegroom was delayed, they all slumbered and slept. [6]But at midnight there was a cry, 'Behold, the bridegroom! Come out to meet him.' [7]Then all those maidens rose and trimmed their lamps. [8]And the foolish said to the wise, 'Give us some of your oil, for our lamps are going out.' [9]But the wise replied, 'Perhaps there will not be enough for us and for you; go rather to the dealers and buy for yourselves. [10]And while they went to buy, the bridegroom came, and those who were ready went in with him to the marriage feast; and the door was shut. [11]Afterward the other maidens came also, saying, 'Lord, lord, open to us.' [12]But he replied, 'Truly, I say to you, I do not know you.' [13]Watch therefore, for you know neither the day nor the hour.''

Matthew 25:1–13

We cannot borrow someone else's faith.

Once again we are listening to Our Lord speaking about the central image and vision of his whole ministry. He is describing yet another aspect of the kingdom of heaven, the ways things are under the rule and will of God. Once again he takes a perfectly familiar scene. Our Lord is the most wonderful practitioner of taking the familiar and ordinary and using it to teach profound truths.

We are at an eastern wedding celebration. Ten young women go out as dusk falls to escort the bridegroom. Five take care to have enough oil in their lamps for a long wait, five do not. When the bridegroom finally arrives they are all asleep. The five with oil to spare are ready quickly. The others ask them for oil but are refused.

As always Jesus is teaching a spiritual truth. The young women stand for all of us who seek what Jesus calls a kingdom, all of us who have come to realize that Our Lord himself can be the source of meaning and purpose in our lives. He is for us the bridegroom we want to welcome into our lives. To find him we have to set out in search. That search is going to take us into some dark places. We are going to need a light to find our way. The first coming of that light can be the urge within us to seek Our Lord in the first place. He himself through the Holy Spirit has actually kindled that light. Our Lord is not some elusive, capricious figure who wants to make it difficult for us to find him; he seeks us too. It is very easy to forget this about Our Lord.

What is the meaning of some having sufficient oil and others not? Is it that Our Lord is saying that we must be realistic about the spiritual journey we are on? Spirituality in a human life does not just happen. It requires effort, time, attention, faithfulness. As with any physical journey we must make preparations, lay in supplies.

Remember how in verse 9 the refusal is expressed. The fact that there is not enough oil for both groups tells us that faith can never be borrowed. Faith must always be a personal possession and there must be a personal commitment to keeping it alight. Faith can certainly be caught from someone else. It can be fanned into flame in us by someone else's love and encouragement, but once it flickers into flame in the lamp of our spirit, it needs a commitment from us to keep it alight. If we are ready to make that commitment our life can be transformed. To possess the light of Christ is to possess something beyond price. That is the Good News for this week.

Sunday between 13 and 19 November

14"For it will be as when a man going on a journey called his servants and entrusted to them his property; 15to one he gave five talents, to another two, to another one, to each according to his ability. Then he went away. 16He who had received the five talents went at once and traded with them; and he made five talents more. 17So also, he who had the two talents made two talents more. 18But he who had received the one talent went and dug in the ground and hid his master's money. 19Now after a long time the master of those servants came and settled accounts with them. 20And he who had received the five talents came forward, bringing five talents more, saying, 'Master, you delivered to me five talents; here I have made five talents more.' 21His master said to him, 'Well done, good and faithful servant; you have been faithful over a little, I will set you over much; enter into the joy of your master.' 22And he also who had the two talents came forward, saying, 'Master, you delivered to me two talents; here I have made two talents more.' 23His master said to him, 'Well done, good and faithful servant; you have been faithful over a little, I will set you over much; enter into the joy of your master.' 24He also who had received the one talent came forward, saying, 'Master, I knew you to be a hard man, reaping where you did not sow, and gathering where you did not winnow; 25so I was afraid, and I went and hid your talent in the ground. Here you have what is yours.' 26But his master answered him, 'You wicked and slothful servant! You knew that I reap where I have not sowed, and gather where I have not winnowed? 27Then you ought to have invested my money with the bankers, and at my coming I should have received what was my own with interest. [28]So take the talent from him, and give it to him who has the ten talents. [29]For to every one who has will more be given, and he will have abundance; but from him who has not, even what he has will be taken away. [30]And cast the worthless servant into the outer darkness; there men will weep and gnash their teeth.''

Matthew 25:14–30

To possess gifts is not enough. We must also have enough trust in God and in ourselves to risk using them.

Again and again Our Lord uses the image of a journey to describe our spiritual experience. He uses it again in this passage. An estate owner is leaving. He leaves some money to each servant to be invested. When the owner returns he asks for an accounting. Each has had a different experience and different results. One by one they report them. Then, in the responses of the estate owner, Our Lord tells us some spiritual truths.

Each of the servants who had invested the money, and had produced more for the employer, was praised. The third servant had not put his share to work. It is worth noting that he did nothing wrong. He didn't steal the money. He didn't lose it. He just did nothing with it. When his sad and shameful tale is told the estate owner takes what that servant had and gives it to the other two.

Let's remind ourselves that Our Lord is using a practical financial situation to illustrate a spiritual truth. The estate owner is God; we are the servants. God gives us the gift of life so that we may serve God in the world of our time. With that gift of life each of us is given certain other gifts. Then comes the question. How are these gifts to be used?

Many factors come into play. Will we have the kind of upbringing which will make us aware of the gifts we possess? Even that does not solve everything. Will we become the kind of person who will risk exercising the gifts we possess? This is a very important point in Jesus' story. All servants were given money. All of us are given gifts. What Our Lord shows us is that it is not enough merely to have gifts. We all know some supremely gifted people whose gifts are imprisioned in a personality which prevents the gifts being used. Our Lord named the greatest imprisoning factor of all, the one that all of us know in some form. Our Lord tells us that the third servant said, "I was afraid." There in that phrase Our Lord names the great enemy of all human gifts — fear. So much is never achieved by so many because of fear.

Notice the consequences. What the timid servant did not put to use was taken from him and given to those who had. Spiritual gifts are no different. Indeed, we might well ask whether any gift is other than spiritual! What God the giver of gifts demands is that we use what is given, that we risk ourselves in trust toward the giving God. The gift itself is not enough. The gift with the added ability to trust is everything. That is the Good News for this week.

The Last Sunday after Pentecost: the Reign of Christ

³¹''When the Son of man comes in his glory, and all the angels with him, then he will sit on his glorious throne. ³²Before him will be gathered all the nations, and he will separate them one from another as a shepherd separates the sheep from the goats, ³³and he will place the sheep at his right hand, but the goats at the left. ³⁴Then the King will say to those at his right hand, 'Come, O blessed of my Father, inherit the kingdom prepared for you from the foundation of the world; ³⁵for I was hungry and you gave me food, I was thirsty and you gave me drink, I was a stranger and you welcomed me, ³⁶I was naked and you clothed me, I was sick and you visited me, I was in prison and you came to me.' ³⁷Then the righteous will answer him, 'Lord, when did we see thee hungry and feed thee, or thirsty and give thee drink? ³⁸And when did we see thee a stranger and welcome thee, or naked and clothe thee? ³⁹And when did we see thee sick or in prison and visit thee?' ⁴⁰And the King will answer them, 'Truly, I say to you, as you did it to one of the least of these my brethren, you did it to me.' ⁴¹Then he will say to those at his left hand, 'Depart from me, you cursed, into the eternal fire prepared for the devil and his angels; ⁴²for I was hungry and you gave me no food, I was thirsty and you gave me no drink, ⁴³I was a stranger and you did not welcome me, naked and you did not clothe me, sick and in prison and you did not visit me.' ⁴⁴Then they also will answer, 'Lord, when did we see thee hungry or thirsty or a stranger or naked or sick or in prison, and did not minister to thee?' ⁴⁵Then he will answer them. 'Truly, I say to you, as you did it not to one of the least of these, you

did it not to me.' [46]And they will go away into eternal punishment, but the righteous into eternal life."

Matthew 25:31–46

Our Lord makes it quite clear that his highest criterion for judging us is whether or not we care and act on that caring.

Every time Our Lord gives us images of the kingdom of heaven he challenges our ideas of what is normal, reasonable, practical. For instance, apply those three words to the idea of loving one's enemies! In this passage he gives us a challenge. He say to us in effect — here is the way things really are; here is what you must decide about. Our Lord then shows us a scene. It's a trial of the whole human race. All are divided into two throngs of people, labelled with two words which have diametrically opposite meanings. One group is called *blessed* [v 34] and the other is called *cursed* [v 41]. There are also two diametrically opposite fates for the two groups. One is offered a kingdom, the other is sent to the fire.

For such radically different things to be meted out to these people it is obvious that they must have behaved in radically different ways. What can be so excellent on the one hand and so awful on the other, as to merit this kind of reward and judgement from God? The answer is made brutally clear in Our Lord's parable. He tells us that the single most important criterion for judging our humanity is that of caring and acting on that care. Someone once said, "The difference is not between those who believe and those who do not believe but between those who care and those who do not care."

Notice how the judge, who is Our Lord, defines the basis of his judgement. We are judged on actions which every one of us is capable of doing [vv 35–36]. We cannot plead that we have not the intellect or the resources to do these things. We can so often persuade ourselves that discerning the will of God for us is complex and mysterious. Some facets of that will may well be complex, but meanwhile the demands of God made on us in this passage are devastatingly simple and clear. Can I feed someone, visit someone, welcome someone, clothe someone? Have there ever been clearer and simpler criteria for following Our Lord?

Notice the surprise of everyone when Our Lord points out that he has been served through our serving of others in his name. Our Lord is telling us again that our relationship with him extends into all our living, all our relationships, all experiences. Somewhere in every moment and place and event he is present, even if he weeps for us in some experiences which we choose. Our Lord is a hidden Lord, always in disguise. Our prayer is that our eyes and ears may be open to know him. That is the Good News for this week.

Other Books by Herbert O'Driscoll

Praying to the Lord of Life: Reflections on the Collects of the Christian Year according to the Book of Alternative Services

A Time for Good News: Reflections on the Gospel for People on the Go

Child of Peace, Lord of Life : Reflections on the Readings of the Common Lectionary

Year A, Volume 1 (from the First Sunday of Advent to the Fifth Sunday in Lent)

Volume 2 (from the Sunday of the Passion to the Last Sunday after Pentecost)

Year B, Volume 1

Year B, Volume 2

Year C, Volume 1

Year C, Volume 2

A Certain Life: Contemporary Meditations on the Way of Christ

Portrait of a Woman: Meditations on the Mother of Our Lord

Crossroads: Times of Decision for the People of God

The Sacred Mirror: Meeting God in Scripture

One Man's Journal: Reflections on Contemporary Living

City Priest, City People: One Man's Journal, Book 2

Books on Spirituality

Soft Bodies in a Hard World: Spirituality for the Vulnerable *by Charles Davis*

Christ Mind, Zen Mind, Child Mind: A Reflection on Zen and Christian Faith and Practice *by John King*

Books on Christian Life

An Open View: Keeping Faith Day by Day *by John Bothwell*

Taking Risks and Keeping Faith: Changes in the Church by *John Bothwell*

New Life: Addressing Change in the Church *by John Bothwell, John Davis, J.C. Fricker, Sheila and George Grant, Dorothy Gregson, Philip Jefferson, Elizabeth Kilbourn*

Light From the East: A Symposium on the Oriental Orthodox and Assyrian Churches *edited by Henry Hill*